EVERY NOW AND THEN

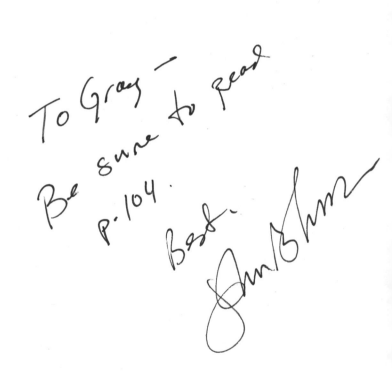

To Gray —
Be sure to read
p. 104.
Best ~

EVERY NOW AND THEN

Occasional Essays

JOHN B. AMOS

Bomari Press

ISBN: 978-0-9798571-0-2

Library of Congress Control Number: 2007905696

Book and cover design: Tabby House

The essays in this collection have been previously
published in the Fredericksburg *Free Lance-Star* or the
Orange County Review and are reprinted with permission
of the managing editors of both newspapers.

Bomari Press
P.O. Box 1175
Orange VA 22960

For my father, M. B. "Fish" Amos

CONTENTS

PREFACE

Three friends offered me good advice.

Friend One: "You ought to write some of this stuff down."

Friend Two: "Put 'em in the local paper. People will tell you what they think, and then you'll know if they're any good."

Friend Three: "Seven hundred-fifty words, max. Five hundred is too short, and people won't read more than 750."

So one evening a few years ago, after dinner, I sat down at my kitchen table and began to write. Six hours later I had drafts of three 750-word essays. The first, titled "Dreaming of Home," begins this collection.

Eventually, *The Orange County Review* began publishing my essays in a weekly column under the heading "Every Now and Then." Since the column's inception I've written about everything from old cars and country music to prize fighting and my mother's cooking. I don't really know how to describe my rather haphazard approach. The best I can come up with is to call these musings "occasional essays."

If there's a recurrent theme here—something that holds otherwise random topics together—it's that remembering matters. I can't quite explain why remembering matters; I just know that it does. Put simply, there are things I don't want to forget: people, places, customs, habits, moments of joy, as well as moments of sadness and loss. These essays are my attempt to keep the past alive. Putting experience down in words gives a measure of permanence to ephemeral memory.

I've enjoyed the writing because it's therapeutic. I've also enjoyed the many kind comments from people who have read my stuff. At first there was a fair amount of puzzlement. "Have you quit your job?" was a frequent question. And, "Don't you have anything better to do?" This one made me laugh because the answer really is, "No."

Old friends have written or called with their own remembrances, offering ideas and stories for future columns. But I've also heard from strangers, who say that the column reminds them of people and places from their own personal pasts. It's gratifying to think that something I've written has struck a chord with others.

Despite the nostalgic tone of *Every Now and Then,* I think I've managed not to be maudlin. I've tried hard not to romanticize or to speak in terms of "the good old days." I admit to being wistful on occasion, but I don't think I'm guilty in these essays of outright sappiness.

Change and progress are subtle. Almost without realizing, we lose sight of The Old amid the onslaught of The New. This I know: Some stuff deserves to be remembered.

And so I write.

J.B.A
JULY 2007

Dreaming of Home

I went by my old house yesterday. I just sat there in the car, watching the workmen as they hammered down flooring for the new porch; and then I got out to take a closer look. The place looks better now than it ever did before: new siding, new windows, new roof, new deck, new everything. My folks never had the money to fix the place up like this, but still they managed to keep it looking pretty good. When Mama died, my dad sold it. It was the right thing to do; but I knew that without my mother to keep it patched together, it would certainly fall to pieces.

Sure enough, within a year or so, the porch roof began to sag. Then the paint began to peel, and an air of general decrepitude set in. A fire a few years ago badly blistered the rear of the house; and since then the words KEEP OUT, emblazoned across the front in florescent orange spray paint, have warned visitors away. So I quit driving by. It was just too sad.

But now a new owner is really fixing the place up.

Yesterday, as I stood leaning up against the rusty,

old fence, watching the carpenters at work, I wanted so badly to go inside to see my home again. One of the workers must have read something in my face because after a few minutes he called out, "Hey, buddy, you wanna go inside?" I accepted, but I'm not really sure I should have.

They'd gutted the entire interior. They'd begun reframing, but from the looks of it, none of the new rooms would be in their old, proper places. The only thing still recognizable to me was the staircase, just inside the front door. I walked upstairs feeling oddly empty, trying to remember what the hallway looked like where my brother and I had played Nerf basketball. I tried to picture the bathroom with the clawfoot tub. Mama's sewing closet. The bunk beds. The window fan I had talked through as a kid to distort my voice. The varnished cedar furniture my parents must have bought soon after they got married. But I couldn't quite picture any of it.

Then back downstairs. My dad's green reading chair? The two oil stoves? The Motorola TV (Had we really kept it in the dining room?) The sofa with the missing leg that Mama kept propped up with a can of peaches? All of it was there in my mind, but none of it was really there, where it was supposed to be.

I stood for a few minutes at a window, looking out at the backyard. Thirty-five years ago it had seemed so big. Big enough to play homerun derby; big enough to clean a stringer full of fish; big enough to split and stack a cord of firewood; big enough for a brick barbecue, several beds of zinnias, a clothesline (over which a kid could hang a sheet to make a tent), a picnic table, and a couple of locust trees; big enough even at one time for a wood-framed summer house. Now, it seemed tiny. I could mow the whole thing in fifteen minutes.

Standing there reminded me of a dream I'd dreamed a couple of years after my mother had died, maybe a year or so after my father had sold the house. In my dream I am standing in the middle of Belleview Avenue. The house is clearly falling apart, and I am distraught. Worried, I walk up onto the porch, but the door is locked. So I peer in through the front window.

My mother is there, wearing a cotton peasant dress, not really like anything she ever wore in real life. She is standing in the middle of the living room floor with a crowbar in her hand, ripping up the floorboards. To my astonishment, she is smiling peacefully, serenely even. For quite some time I stand there, in my dream, watching her as she pulls up board after board and tosses them out the side window. Every so often she looks at me and gently smiles. She never actually says the words, but I know she is telling me just to let the old place go.

I'm working on it.

Doc Savage, Man of Bronze

I figured they had put me in the dumb class by accident. I was in the sixth grade, and all the smart, cool kids were down in the other wing of the building as part of some newfangled "team teaching" experiment. Somehow I got stuck in a traditional classroom with none of my friends. It proved to be a lonesome year, redeemed only by my discovery of *Doc Savage, Man of Bronze*.

Once a week my English teacher allowed us free time to read whatever we wanted. I'm sure she hoped I would choose quality classics or the kind of Newberry Award winners she was always reading aloud to us. However, after I found *Doc Savage*, nothing else could compare.

Doc was part Superman, part Tarzan, and part Sherlock Holmes. He fought evil in the shadowy underworld of big city criminals. To a boy, how could literary merit compete with the dark seediness of a *Doc Savage* adventure? It couldn't.

I didn't know it at the time, but these novels had

first appeared in the 1930s and were classics of pulp fiction: dime novels printed on cheap pulp paper with eye-popping covers. The classic pulps included such long-running magazines as *Amazing Stories, The Shadow, Captain Future,"* and, of course, *Doc Savage*.

Just a glance at their lurid covers (with one-eyed aliens attacking scantily clad, buxom beauties; and bulbous spaceships disgorging giant spiders onto our unsuspecting Earth) let you know that pulps were the cream of lowbrow literature.

In the late 1960s, just as I was hitting middle school, someone got the idea to update the *Doc Savage* books. The stories themselves, I think, remained as they had first appeared in the '30s; but the covers were modernized, adopting a sort of James Bond-as-Rambo look. The "new" Doc wore a sleeveless safari vest with a cartridge belt full of ammunition slung across his chest. He stared coolly out at the reader, his massive arms crossed Schwarzenegger-style, an automatic weapon hanging at his side.

The stories inside didn't really match the covers, but so what? Anybody who's ever read the teaser on the front of a comic book knows that covers are designed merely to catch the reader's interest. The updated *Doc Savage* certainly caught mine.

So, I spent all my free reading time on titles like *The Green Eagle, The Mindless Monsters,* and *Cold Death.*

I will always be grateful to Mrs. Burnett for letting me read these cheesy things. Even back then, I must have realized that *Doc Savage* books bordered on the illicit. Many teachers would have strongly discouraged kids from reading such stuff at school. Many would have tagged these books as "trash" or banned them outright. But this most traditional of teachers, this gray-haired minister's wife who tolerated no nonsense, turned a blind eye and let me keep on reading.

She was one wise woman, and she understood boys. Pretty soon, she began to pass along copies of things she liked (and things she thought would be good for me). I especially remember *Up a Road Slowly* and *Light in the Forest*, quality teen lit with strong moral messages. I read them and liked them, but I would never even have cracked their covers had she tried to squash my interest in the Man of Bronze.

A *Washington Post* article recently argued that young boys resist reading because books of heroic action have gradually been nudged out of the curriculum. Biographies, war stories and adventures on the high seas have been replaced with things like *Sarah Plain and Tall* and *Julie of the Wolves*. These are perfectly good books, but (at the risk of sounding sexist) they ain't no *Doc Savage*. I don't blame boys for not wanting to read them.

In reality, however, it's not just boys that don't read anymore; it's people in general. Reading today is under siege from a pervasive, insidious video culture. Kids and adults alike satisfy their craving for action stories not with books, but with images from television, movies and electronic games. Who wants to expend effort reading about heroes fighting villains when, with a few clicks on the computer, you can actually be the hero who defeats the villain?

Like Doc Savage himself, I sometimes feel as if I'm up against the amassed forces of evil. I keep hoping that, like Doc, I can win this battle. But as of now, it looks pretty grim. The bad guys are winning.

CARS THAT MATTER

I'm not a car nut. I've never understood the debate between Ford and Chevy. If you put me in front of a line of ten cars, all different makes and models, and told me to identify them, I'm sure I'd flunk the test. When kids in my class start talking about the latest in "cool" cars, I just tune them out. I've never loved a car enough to keep it washed and waxed regularly. The fact is, I'm just not very particular. When it comes to cars, give me something that runs and I'm happy.

Still, some cars have mattered.

My dad's 1960 Chevrolet Impala mattered. It was the only brand-new car he ever owned. I'm not sure if it was a selling feature of that particular model, or just a quirk peculiar to his car alone, but you could start it without the key. Though I don't really know automobiles, I still stop by the local classic car shows occasionally, hoping to see one like it, battleship gray with horizontal tail fins.

Later, his 1968 Ford Galaxy with the bad flywheel mattered. Even though I don't know what a flywheel is or what a flywheel does, I do know this: a flywheel with missing teeth means that the car won't start, and you must move the flywheel to a place where there are no missing teeth. On more than one occasion, I had to get under the hood and manually turn the flywheel in order to get the car to start. It was sort of like starting an old-fashioned biplane by physically spinning the propeller. I always felt that I should be wearing pilot's goggles, a Red Baron scarf, and yelling "Contact!" when driving the Galaxy.

The 1974 Ford Pinto hatchback with the huge Flaming Pinto Head decal on the hood really mattered. It was the first car I ever bought with my own money. I borrowed 1,400 dollars from National Bank and Trust and made ninety-nine dollar payments until it was paid off. I have a picture of my wife and me leaving for our honeymoon in it. Dark green exterior with flaming racing stripes down the sides. Tin cans tied to the back, and a sign (courtesy of the groomsmen) that reads: MIGRANT FARM WORKERS, HEADING SOUTH.

Some cars, of course, haven't mattered at all. I'd just as soon forget the maroon AMC Matador that broke down on my way to trade it in. Same goes for the Oldsmobile station wagon that ended up painted Crest Toothpaste blue. When you ask for a cheap paint job, you get a cheap paint job.

The car that matters most, however, was The Morris. Officially, it was a 1958 Morris Minor 1000, an English car resembling a VW Beetle that my dad bought third-hand for five hundred dollars. The first thing he did was put stickers of leaping bass on the rear end; the second thing he did was to install homemade brackets on the roof to hold the fishing poles. Though he bought it exclusively as a fishing car, it ended up being much more than that. I drove it to my senior prom, and I drove it religiously to Lake of the Woods when dating my wife-to-be. During the worst of the mid-'70s gas crisis, we were the only people around with a car that got more than thirty miles per gallon (an advantage offset somewhat by the fact that you had to give it a quart of oil every two or three days).

It didn't matter that the hood might fly up while you were driving. It didn't matter that the interior upholstery was nonexistent. It didn't matter that the headlights were unreliable. Once, at the end of an all-day fishing trip when the lights wouldn't work, my brother and I leaned out the window holding flashlights on the gravel road so my father could see to drive back to town. None of this mattered because The Morris had character.

They say that dog owners eventually come to resemble their dogs. I think the same may be true of car owners. For sure, a car provides insight into a person's character and personality. What does it say about me that I drive a tired, old, gray Nissan pickup with almost 200,000 miles on it? Obviously, that I am tired, old, gray, and in not such good shape. Still, I'm not ready to get rid of it. It's just beginning to develop a bit of character.

COOKIN' QUICK

Mama put the turkey in the bathtub. She had to. Thanksgiving was only a day away, and she'd burned the first bird in the microwave. Microwave technology was still pretty new, and she thought preparing Thanksgiving dinner might be less hassle if she could cook the turkey quickly. It didn't work. I didn't actually see the result, but she said it wasn't pretty. So she had to thaw another; and as things were busy in the kitchen, the bathtub seemed the most logical place.

My mother was not the least bit ditzy. In fact, she was by far the most stable, practical, and sensible person I ever knew. But when it came to cooking, she valued two things above all: speed and economy. Make it quick and make it cheap.

I'm sure microwave turkey only crossed her mind because she thought it might save her a few hours. Her specialties were things like Watergate Salad (four ingredients and two minutes prep time), Jumbo Raisin Cookies (yield: ten dozen, cost: about two bucks), broccoli and Cheez Whiz casserole (one of a thousand recipes calling for Campbell's cream of celery soup), and a variety of Bisquick Impossible Pies (Bisquick: the prime staple for cooking cheap).

I'm not complaining, mind you. I liked most everything she cooked: even navy beans with stewed tomatoes, which somehow always happened to be on the menu when our minister, Mr. Binns, dropped by.

I guess I would call my mother a responsible cook. She never fed us from frozen packages, and she was always looking for good, new things to feed her family. She didn't hesitate to experiment; and usually her experiments were successful, or at least passable. (She once bottled her own homemade ketchup. I remember it as thin and runny, but flavorful. Baked Spam with melted American cheese slices, however, was a serious mistake.)

My mother never actually said it, but I always got the impression that, for her, cooking was a necessary evil. There were times she loved it—especially around Christmas when she made date pinwheel cookies and chocolate-covered peanut butter candy. But more often than not, she regarded cooking as just something that needed doing, a required sacrifice in the ritual of her life.

Plenty of other things competed for her time and attention—things like vacuuming, making beds, dusting, sweeping, emptying ashtrays, scrubbing and waxing floors, washing clothes, hanging them on the line, and ironing. I suppose if she'd ever had a maid, my mother might have been a better cook.

And her jobs changed with the seasons: planting zinnias in the spring, painting the house in the summer, raking leaves in the fall, sealing the windows with plastic in the winter, and watching for bargains at the grocery store the whole year round.

All of this was in addition to the things she really loved doing: reading, sewing, dancing with my father, checking on my grandparents, and entertaining her grandkids (She once made my nephew a "real" Professional Rasslin' belt).

Add to this her job as an aide in a special-ed class at the high school, where her title could easily have been "assistant mother," and it's easy to understand why she pushed cooking to the back burner.

My mother moved through the world with amazing grace. If the word "dashing" can be applied to women, she was a dashing woman. Tall, elegant, and vibrantly alive, Jean Colvin Amos lived life with striking beauty. No one walked with such confidence. No one smiled with such goodness. No one put on fewer airs. She was a natural at living. When she died in 1989 at the age of fifty-eight, the world lost some of its spark.

Soon after she died, I found a scrapbook full of recipes that she'd collected from friends and cut out from newspapers and magazines. Many are for exotic dishes that I know she never tried; but many give directions for the standards that came from my mother's kitchen: things like squash casserole, copper carrots, apple crisp, and banana pudding.

One recipe—for cranberry-nut bread—I particularly cherish. Beside it, written in my mother's hand, is a note that reads, "John likes this." Among other ingredients, it calls for a tablespoon of orange peel. In typical fashion, my mother has crossed out "peel" and substituted "juice." It's a lot quicker to squeeze an orange than to peel it.

Note to Mama: I never knew the difference.

Love, John.

Do You Believe in Magic?

Picture a large, open attic.

A cluster of teenagers stands around a pool table in the corner, laughing and joking, occasionally passing the cue stick from one to another. A few feet away, two girls click and clack their way through an intense game of air hockey. Back in the shadows, boys in stocking caps twirl away at the Foosball table.

Others just lounge, flopped out on frayed old sofas and oversized stuffed chairs. Periodically they check their cell phones. Several sit on the floor, knees pulled up to their chins, chatting.

A girl standing on a chair writes a note in pink chalk on a wall of stylized graffiti.

Above all the clamor and commotion, music rises. Sweet, sweet music.

Not canned tunes spun by a DJ. Not CDs from a boom box— real, live music. Played in the flesh by kids (and a few adults) who are testing their musical wings.

The musicians come as they are: with trumpets, guitars, violins, keyboards and drums. Some are novices without much confidence. Others are old hands in search of a place to meet fellow musicians. All of them are looking for the same thing: they just want to make music.

It's Friday night, and this is The Orange Jam.

To the untrained eye, The Jam may seem like just another typical teen hangout. Not so. Not so at all. This is more than just a place for teenagers to gather. More than just a small-town attempt to keep kids off the street and out of trouble. Something's happening here. Something special. Something real.

And that something has mostly to do with John Kiefer, owner of a small local music store and guru to dozens of budding musicians.

To watch this man orchestrate the chaos that is The Jam is to witness firsthand the liberating and transforming power of live music.

Part teacher and part coach; part stream-of-consciousness comedian and part musical evangelist, John Kiefer has the rare ability to get kids to listen, to think, to try, and to believe in themselves.

Personally, I love listening to music; but I don't really understand it, at least not in a technical sense. I do, however, know good teaching when I see it; and I've never seen better than John in action on a Friday night.

The best teachers haven't forgotten what it was like to be a kid. In fact, the really good ones have remained kids themselves at heart. They share their passions with a kind of innocent zeal that borders on missionary fervor.

John sings and plays guitar with childlike abandon, with a sort of reckless, inspired fury that's contagious. Everyone around him catches the bug. It's not an act. He sings and plays because the music just has to get out.

Fact: Most adults have had music beaten out of them. Life has grown serious. No time to sing. No time to play. Gotta run. Gotta make a buck.

A scene from a recent Jam stands in stark contrast to this "dead-to-music" mentality: On a small platform a few boys play "Red House" by Jimi Hendrix. Another kid jumps from the sofa, grabs his trumpet and joins in. Suddenly, the trumpet ain't just for the marching band anymore. It's cool and soulful. In the back of the room, standing atop a table, a middle-aged music teacher in baggy pants and an orange baseball cap dances, lost in the music. He's a kid again. Or maybe he just never grew up.

Think for a moment about what you most desire for your children? You want them to become confident and independent. You want them to be generous and considerate of others. You want them to think before they act, to take risks without putting themselves in danger. You want their brains to be active. You want them actually to do something, not just to hang around the house being bored. You want them to be open and friendly, inclusive rather than exclusive. You want them comfortable around people, not sullen, disaffected loners. You want them to learn from their mistakes. But mostly, you want them to be happy and to feel deeply the joy of living. You want their souls to sing.

Now think about what happens when a group of kids pick up their instruments and step on stage to play for an audience. It's everything you hope for them. It's magic.

Do you believe? I do.

YES, BUT IS IT ART?

I love modern art.

I know lots of people think it's bogus. They see a paint-splattered canvas and respond with a skeptical, "Any fool could do that." I understand. I used to think the same way. But then I was converted.

Here's my story: The sun was sinking. My feet hurt. I'd been strolling aimlessly through the museum for hours. If I didn't find something soon, the day would be a total loss. So in desperation I headed for the Hirshhorn, a concrete doughnut of a building, located on the National Mall in D.C. and filled with outrageously "out there" stuff. I'd been avoiding the place all day.

I was a fourth-year student at the University of Virginia, and I was on a mission. I'd taken a class in art history, and the only graded assignment was to visit an art museum, find an interesting work, and write an essay interpreting it. So one spring day I found myself wandering the National Gallery, looking for something to write about.

The choice to visit this particular museum was intentional. I had foolishly (and somewhat arrogantly) made up my mind to look only at "traditional art." I'm not even sure what I meant by that term, other than that I had some vague notion of liking old better than new. So all day I had confined myself to the West Wing of the Gallery, home of the masters: daVinci, Rembrandt, and the like.

Surely, if I had to write about a work of art, I could find something in this stately gallery full of religious paintings, landscapes, still lifes, and classical sculptures. I had no intention of wasting my day on abstract, modern, weird stuff. But the more I looked, the less I seemed to see.

And now time was running out. I still hadn't found a suitable subject for the essay; so, on a lark, into the Hirshhorn I went.

The place was filled with the bizarre, the odd, the outlandish: huge canvases of floating colored blocks; garish paintings that seemed more related to geometry than art; sculptures of tossed-together wires and brushes; thinly pressed panes of beeswax stamped with random images. These artists, eager to push the limits of what defines art, were mostly out to shock. Much in the museum I didn't understand, and much I didn't really care to understand.

I was just about ready to dismiss the whole place as a fun but essentially silly joke when something caught my eye that knocked me, metaphorically speaking, head over heels.

A small sculpture titled *City Square,* by Alberto Giacometti, stood on a stand in the second-floor exhibition hall. Though cast in bronze, the piece gave the impression of clay. Several tiny, elongated human stick-figures looked as if they'd been pulled up from the mire by an invisible creating hand. They strode across the rectangular base, as if hurrying off to some crucial, but pointless business meeting. They didn't carry briefcases, but they very well could have.

What fascinated me most were their feet. Huge in relation to the extended torsos, they seemed forever locked to the earth, though their bodies were being pulled up to heaven.

Contradictions abounded: earthen men stretching skyward, stillness in motion, purposeless purpose. These figures, simultaneously ridiculous and dignified, looked a bit like a kid's pipe-cleaner creations; but somehow they struck me as exquisitely human.

From that moment on, I have tried to keep my mind open to modern art. And I've come to regard the Hirshhorn as one of my favorite places. I love the outdoor sculpture garden (*The Prophet* especially), and I never tire of being confronted by fresh, offbeat takes on the world from artists I've never heard of.

I still don't "get" all of it (the exhibit of stuffed animals tacked to the wall didn't really do much for me). But "getting it" isn't the point. If someone wants to spend his life creating art out of fluorescent lightbulbs—as does Dan Flavin, whose work I saw on a recent trip—who am I to fuss? I don't have to like it, but I don't have to dismiss it either.

Art enriches life. But only if we're open to it. I don't quite understand the mystery of how this happens. I just know that it does.

Turkish Delight

Like so many Americans, I am geographically illiterate. I take no pride in saying so, but the plain truth is: I don't know much about other places. I'm pretty much a homebody; and as such, I've never pushed myself to learn. I know the basics—the fifty states, the seven continents, the Atlantic and Pacific Oceans—but beyond that, my knowledge is kind of shaky. Along with classical music, geography remains one of the great gaping holes in my own education.

But I'm trying. And gradually I'm learning.

Let's talk Turkey.

Had you asked me six months ago to tell you everything I know about Turkey, you'd probably have gotten a blank stare in response. Or, even worse, you might have gotten a collection of rank stereotypes and misperceptions—something along the lines of, "It's one of those really dangerous Middle East countries where they all wear turbans, carry sabers, ride camels, and hate Americans."

Ask me the same question today, and I could do

better. A ten-day trip down the western coast of Turkey, paid for by a school that takes the education of its students and faculty seriously, has dispelled all stereotypes and opened my eyes. In ten short days I fell in love with the place. I'd go back tomorrow if I could.

Here are some lasting images. I write them now as remembrances in case I don't get the chance to go back:

Removing my shoes as I step into Istanbul's Blue Mosque, which reminds me that some people in the world still cherish the idea of sacred space.

Cruising the Bosporus, the narrow strait that divides two continents, thinking about our guide's comment that Turkey is a "schizophrenic" country—its identity split between Europe and Asia.

Gazing out the hotel window at 2:00 in the morning, mesmerized by the half moon that hangs over the Bosporus.

Laughing at the shop owner in the Grand Bazaar who calls out, "Hey, American man, come into my shop and buy something you do not need."

Hearing the call to prayer from a fifteenth century Moslem mosque as I stand amid the ruins of a sixth century Christian church.

Weeping at seeing the mosaics in the Church of St. Savior in Chora, overwhelmed by the thought that we skeptical moderns have barely a clue as to the faith that produced such work.

Watching Aegean blue turn to "wine-dark seas" at sunset.

I saw things on this trip I never believed I'd see. And I thought thoughts I never thought I'd think. But most unexpected was that I returned home having made a new Turkish friend. So, let me tell you a bit about Yahya.

Yahya Kemal Cinar is forty-eight years old and for the past sixteen years has worked as a guide for tourist groups visiting Turkey. It's hard to imagine anyone better suited to his job.

The man is a teacher extraordinaire.

For ten days his lectures cut a swath across 4,000 years of history and half a dozen cultures. He spoke with ease on topics ranging from Greek and Roman architecture to World War I battle strategies at Gallipoli to religious practices of the Ottoman Turks. His knowledge of dates was encyclopedic. His ability to give background and context to historical events was beyond impressive. When I asked how he knew so much about so much, he simply commented, "There's always something more to learn."

And he was equally well-versed in current events. A brief note from my journal gives a sense of his love and concern for modern Turkey: "Yahya spoke today with great passion about Turkey's relationship with the United States, about America's role in the world, and about Turkey's ambivalence at the prospect of joining the European Union. His pride in his country is palpable. I wish Americans were as informed about their own country as this man is about his."

Though he has no children of his own, Yahya is a natural with high school students. A wink, a wry smile, and a penchant for silliness are his tools for connecting with kids. He'd make an outstanding classroom teacher, but my sense is that he'd feel frustrated and confined. His real genius is bringing history alive on the road. The classroom would cramp his style.

I doubt that I'll ever get back to Turkey. So for now I can only pass along Yahya's parting message: "Tell your friends back home to come to Turkey."

And so I have.

PREACHING SUNDAY

If you dropped your quarter, it stood a good chance of rolling all the way to the front of the church. That's why every Sunday, when my dad gave me money for the collection plate, I clutched it with both hands.

The few times I did accidentally drop it, everything moved in slow motion: I'd be tossing a coin distractedly from palm to palm when suddenly it would leap from my hand like a live thing, hit the floor with a clink, and then begin its stately, jangling roll down the uncarpeted center aisle. I'd duck my head, embarrassed, while every head in church turned to discover the culprit. Even the portrait of Jesus kneeling in prayer that hung above the pulpit seemed to aim its gaze at me.

My dropped coins usually happened on "Preaching Sundays." That's because on those days I more than likely had two quarters: one for Sunday school and another for worship. A boy can only hold two quarters for so long without dropping at least one.

"Preaching Sunday" is a phenomenon unique to small, rural churches. My family attended Lower Rapidan Baptist, a little stone church just across the river a few hundred yards into Culpeper County. Such a small church couldn't afford its own minister, so we joined with two other tiny congregations—Cedar Run and Crooked Run—to hire the Reverend Floyd T. Binns.

Because Mr. Binns couldn't be in three places at once, he created a complicated schedule of "Preaching Sundays." By conducting an early service at 10:00, then hustling off to one of the other churches, he was able to guarantee each congregation at least two full worship services per month. On "off" Sundays we simply held Sunday school for an hour and went home. Naturally, the first thing you asked upon waking up Sunday morning was, "Is today a Preaching Sunday?"

A typical morning at Lower Rapidan began with Sunday school.

My grandfather would announce an opening hymn (The hope I heard as a boy in songs like "In the Garden," "My Faith Looks Up to Thee," and "Toiling On" remains with me still.) Accompanied by Aunt Lavie on organ, we'd sing. Then granddaddy would lead us in a responsive reading from the Psalms, say a prayer, and dismiss the congregation to its various classes.

Adults remained in the main part of the sanctuary, taught by my father; teens moved with my Aunt Myrtle to the side pews at the front of the church; and children headed to the vestibule so that their noise wouldn't disturb the others. The church functioned essentially as a one-room schoolhouse.

Once Mr. Binns arrived, the worship service could begin.

Baptist preachers are sometimes stereotyped as hellfire-and-damnation Bible thumpers. Floyd Binns was not that. A man of uncommon dignity, he lived a straightforward and uncompromising faith. His sermons were models of organization, delivered in an unadorned, reserved style. He believed in and taught the importance of clear thinking, freedom of conscience, and civic duty. Unlike so many hotshot celebrity preachers today, he believed fiercely in the separation of church and state. He was constitutionally incapable of manipulative emotionalism or cheap religious fervor.

In addition to serving forty-plus years as minister for three churches, he also taught high school government, coached baseball at Mitchell's, girls' softball at Culpeper High, and served as chaplain for countless community organizations. *Ripley's "Believe It or Not"* actually wrote about him once in its Sunday comic, marveling at the sheer number of activities he involved himself in.

That article failed to mention, of course, that among his other duties, Mr. Binns was also my father's hero. I'm sure he served in that unofficial capacity for many other young men and women whose lives he touched so deeply. The school that now bears his name ought always to honor the legacy of this robust, vigorous, faithful man.

As a teenager I suppose I "outgrew" Lower Rapidan Baptist. My parents never insisted that I continue on there. As long I went to church somewhere, they were satisfied.

Though I'm Episcopalian now, I know that my roots are really in the old stone Baptist church by the river. It steeped me in the stories of the Bible, the great hymns of faith, and the witness of family who came each Sunday to work and worship. I learned without knowing I was learning. And I believed without knowing I was believing. There are a lot worse things that could happen to a kid.

SWEET TALK FROM TENNESSEE

I really couldn't believe my ears. I'm from the South, but I'd never heard a drawl quite like this before. I turned and found myself confronted by a skinny little eight-year-old blonde kid in a purple-flowered bathing suit, speaking the accents of heaven.

Her two tiny friends stood beside her, sassy, hands on their hips, wanting to know what I was up to.

Here's the story: Even at the beach, I take my work seriously. I don't just play in the sand. I design. I build. I sculpt.

For most of the week the surf had pounded the coast, cutting a deep gouge into the shoreline. A waist-high wall of hard, packed sand ran several hundred feet in both directions down the beach. Normally, I specialize in vertical structures—castles, mountains, deep holes, and the like—but the sand-shelf gave me a rare opportunity to practice in the horizontal mode.

Each morning, along with towels and chairs, sun-screen and umbrellas, I'd bring a knife and spoon with me to the beach, my sculptor's utensils for carving fantastical shapes into the face of the wall.

As the days passed, my carvings grew ever more elaborate. By week's end, I had graduated from simple stairs, doors, bridges and arches to something much more exotic. My final creation was a kind of sideways totem pole. I cut into the beach-ledge the rugged face of a crowned king, a setting sun, a diving eagle, a leaping whale, lightning bolts, all manner of abstract curlicues and vaguely symbolic doodlings.

As I put the finishing touches on this masterpiece, the question came from behind me. "Ya'll's the ones been buildin' all them curvy thangs up and down the beach?"

Startled, not just by an unexpected visitor but by the drawliest of Southern drawls, I turned and said, "Child, where in the world are you from?"

"Tazwell, Tennessee," came the prompt reply. "I'm Luanne. These here are Ruth Anne and Gabrielle."

That little snippet of conversation has stuck in my mind for more than a decade now, a pure reminder of the innocent beauty of Southern speech. I've never been to Tazwell, Tennessee; but if everybody there speaks like Luanne, someday I must.

In an essay titled "The Search for Southern Identity," historian C. Vann Woodward describes our Southern heritage as "an old hunting jacket." We slip it on comfortably, he says, when we're at home; but when we venture abroad, we exchange it for "more conventional garb." His point is that many Southerners aren't entirely comfortable with their Southernness. It's fine among friends, but we're a little uneasy outside the confines of home.

In the 1950s speech courses grew quite popular among Southerners who had moved up North. Such classes aimed at helping businessmen lose—or at least disguise—their accents. A drawl or a twang, it seems, wasn't sophisticated, wasn't educated, and certainly wasn't good for business.

In the media also, a Southern accent became a sure-fire sign of backwardness. Even today, can you think of a single national newscaster with a Southern lilt?

Woodward, whose essay appeared in 1958, talked about the South being in danger of losing its identity. As he claimed, we're blending "inconspicuously into the national pattern." Certainly, his fears have largely been realized in the four-and-a-half decades since he first voiced them. For sure, today's South is a different, less distinctive place than it was in my youth.

When I first met her on the beach, Luanne was only eight years old. She didn't think—probably because no one had ridiculed her yet—that her accent was hillbilly. I hope to goodness in the time since that she hasn't been made to feel self-conscious or awkward or ignorant because of it.

And I hope she hasn't done what I've done.

I grew up pronouncing the words "out" and "about" as "oat" and "a-boat." "South" and "mouth" became "soath" and "moath." "Mouse" and "house" received similar treatment. But over time, especially around non-Southerners, I started pronouncing these words more "normally." Today, as Woodward says, I slip easily into the accent of my youth when I'm at home. But away from the comfort and safety of family, I tend to trade the speech of my childhood for some-

43

thing blander and less uniquely Southern. It's not a conscious thing, but it happens.

Whenever I catch myself backsliding, I think of Luanne, the little girl on the beach with the gorgeous Tennessee drawl.

THE DEVIL'S PICTURE BOOK

Fifteen-two, fifteen-four, fifteen-six; two for a pair makes eight. Six more for 'trips," two for 'his nibs,' and one for 'last card.' Plus, I still have the crib."

This is the language of cribbage, a game my father taught me during my junior year in high school. Like most card games, it's addictive. For a while, we played every evening: me sitting on the floor, my dad in his reading chair smoking a pipe, and the board situated on the end table between us.

Cribbage: the king of all counting games—a card game so cool it not only has its own lingo, it even has its own special pegboard for keeping score. You could tally up the points just as easily on a piece of paper, but it wouldn't be the same. Cribbage is nothing without the board. The best cribbage boards are works of art, rivaling backgammon boxes in their beauty.

It's a good thing I didn't grow up back in the days when cards were considered sinful. I'd be going to Hell, for sure, because I love playing with "the Devil's Picture Book." I was introduced early to the joys of card playing; and in turn I taught my own children early on how to shuffle, how to deal, and how to calculate. They most certainly are not shuffling, dealing, or calculating people; but friendly family competition at cards has helped to make and keep them sharp. In fact, on the list of essential parenting tools, I'd put "deck of playing cards" at the very top.

Truth is, some of my favorite moments in life have involved card games.

When I was a kid, cards meant couples: Basil and Martha, Carroll and Lois, Melvin and Jean. I can still hear my parents' laughter as they sat with their friends around our kitchen table, playing Setback or Pinochle. My folks weren't moviegoers, and they weren't attendees on the cocktail circuit. Rather, their idea of a pleasant evening was simple: good friends, good conversation, a tray of crackers and cheese, and the double-deck intricacies of a game of Canasta.

Later, as a senior at Orange County High School, I courted my future wife in this way: I'd get off work at the drug store around 9:00, hop in the car and drive forty-five minutes to her house, then spend the next hour flopped out in the living room floor playing Double Russian Solitaire while listening to Dylan and Springsteen albums. Later, I'd race back to town just in time to make midnight curfew. Love's a funny thing.

In college, at the University of Virginia, I spent hours in the dorm playing Spades, Hearts, and all manner of Poker with my roommates. I watched incredulously one evening as a friend almost lost his fiancé by dropping the Queen of Spades on her at an inopportune time during a game of Cutthroat. And I'm pretty sure my GPA would have been significantly better had I not spent so much time playing Acey-Deucey.

College is also where I learned such exotic card games as Rat Fink and Casino. These I've intentionally passed on to my own children, hoping that they'll do the same for theirs someday.

Rat Fink is short game of tricks and trumps, with rules so arcane they almost defy reason. Casino, a fast-paced counting game with eleven points per deck, is fun because it both rewards and punishes risk. A normal game of Casino ends at twenty-one, but I recently played a marathon with my son to a thousand (It took me the better part of a month, but finally I beat him).

So much of modern entertainment is electronic. Video games, DVDs, digital this and downloaded that. Video golf, on-line chess, even digitized hunting. We live in a virtual age where "real don't matter."

The ultimate sacrilege: computerized card games like Microsoft Hearts, Spider Solitaire and on-line Poker. Don't get me wrong. Such games are fun, and they're every bit as addictive as the real thing. But that's the tragedy. Actual human opponents are no longer necessary.

Fact: a card game's not a card game without somebody to talk to across the table.

I get so tired of fighting "progress." It's enough to get a body down. Sometimes I just want to do like Elvis: take a pistol and blast away at the next screen I see. Blow it to kingdom come.

My soul craves low-tech. Just give me a deck of cards, a tray of crackers, and thou.

THE HUMAN TOUCH

Four decades of change can be summed up this way: we've lost the human touch. I could list a million ways that life in this small town is different now. But it all comes down to the simple fact that we're less personal in our dealings with one another. To be fair, it's not just Orange that has suffered this change. Everything everywhere feels more disconnected and alien to me. Life today is simply less neighborly.

I suppose, if we wanted to lay blame, we could start with the "disappearing Main Street" phenomenon. Downtown Orange during the mid-1960s sounds like something from another world. In my youth Main Street boasted two department stores, three drug stores with lunch counters, an upscale men's clothing shop, two furniture stores, a stationer, a grocer that made home deliveries, a butcher shop, a jeweler, an optometrist, two hardware stores, a Five and Dime, a movie theater, two banks, two pool halls, a service station, a train depot, and a liquor store.

These businesses were all owned or operated by

local folks. The people who sat next to you in church were the same people who doctored your kids, sold you your washing machine, filled your gas tank, and offered your teenage children summer jobs. When you shopped, you weren't just getting the stuff you needed; you also were visiting neighbors.

When I was a kid, the great Saturday pastime was collecting bottles. We'd spend the morning rummaging around the neighborhood looking for glass soda bottles to cash in for two cents apiece. It took a full morning's work and a wagonload of bottles to yield enough cash to buy a decent amount of penny candy. Around noon we'd roll the wagon through the doors of the Safeway, right up to the manager's window. We'd unload the bottles, collect the cash, and then hightail it to the Frozen Custard store on Madison Road, where we'd spend every cent on Pixie Stix, Peanut Butter Logs, and Mary Janes.

Remarkable as it sounds now, we weren't a bother to anyone. The Safeway manager knew us, and he knew our parents. He valued and rewarded our resourcefulness. Can you imagine such a scenario in today's supermarket?

Then there was the Hostess man. I never knew his name, but once a week he'd drive a postal-type, open-door delivery truck through our neighborhood taking orders for bread, cakes, pies, and other snacks. If I managed to catch him at the stop sign, he'd let me hop in and ride the rest of the way down the block. As he pulled up to our house to take the weekly order, he'd sneak me a package of cupcakes with orange icing. Time was when a child's life was full of contact with such adults, people who weren't really family but who treated you like family anyway.

I recently spotted a signboard in front of a local business exhorting us all to SHOP ORANGE FIRST. That's a tough sell. Long ago Wal-Mart, Target, Lowe's, The Home Depot, and a thousand other suburban megastores beckoned; and we all heeded their siren song. Of course, what we gained in selection, we sacrificed in community. And what we saved in dollars, we lost in personal connection. To my mind, it wasn't an even trade.

The personal touch wasn't just confined to retail businesses. Take Dr. Warren, for instance. When I came down with pneumonia one Halloween night—I was maybe six years old—my mother hustled me off to his house on Blue Ridge Drive. It didn't matter that she had interrupted his weekly poker game (at least not much). She called, and then she took me to his house where he examined me, prescribed penicillin, and then returned to his card game. I'm sure medical care today is far better, but the system isn't nearly so humane.

To me the small town personal touch was best embodied in someone like Henry Wilson. An employee of the Town maintenance crew, Henry's job for much of the '70s and '80s was sweeping the street. All day long he'd push his cart up and down Main Street, sweeping the gutters and jawing with local passersby. Hard to believe we were once a town willing to pay an elderly gentleman a salary just for keeping the curb clean.

A friend recently wrote me a note saying, "Many of us remember a town and a countryside lost to questionable progress." I know exactly what she means.

THE MAN IN BLACK

*I've seen the Mona Lisa, I've heard Shakespeare
spoke real fine;
Just like hearing Johnny Cash sing "I Walk the
Line."*
—Rodney Crowell

Lo, and behold! My teenage daughter has decided she likes country music. Two years ago, she wouldn't have been caught dead listening to anything with a twang. But now, for some reason, Kenny Chesney, Keith Urban, Tim McGraw and the like are cool. I've listened, and most of it is okay. But it's hard to believe that in twenty years the current crop of Nashville sensations will be remembered as anything more than just a bunch of empty cowboy hats.

Picture this: *A crisp day in early December. Two small boys, one ten and the other six. They are raking leaves. Their old-lady neighbor has promised to pay them three dollars each if they rake the entire yard. They finish and race to the door. She counts out six one-dollar bills into their outstretched hands and gives them each a doughnut, for a job well done. They race three blocks "uptown" to the drugstore and go straight to the record bin where they find, right in front,* Johnny Cash: Live at Folsom Prison. *$4.88. That's two days worth of raking leaves, but they don't hesitate. It's only a few weeks until Christmas, and this is a present for their father. By tradition, everyone in the family gets to open one present on Christmas Eve, and the boys will make sure that their father opens this one.*

Almost four decades later that album remains something extraordinary. Singing in front of a crowd of inmates who obviously regard him as one of their own, the Man in Black rips through a set of hard-core songs aimed straight at this captive audience of desperate men. Just a glance at the titles lets you know he's performing for a tough crowd: "Folsom Prison Blues," "Busted," "Dark as the Dungeon," "Cocaine Blues," and "Long Black Veil." Even as a kid, I knew something was happening when Johnny Cash sang, "I shot a man in Reno just to watch him die," and the inmates roared their approval (Kind of a strange Christmas present, now that I think about it).

Johnny Cash was—and is—the real deal. When he died, the tributes to his life and music were glowing. Raul Malo: "Johnny Cash is the Mount Rushmore of music." Bob Dylan: "It's like a voice from the middle of the earth." Bono: "Every man knows he is a sissy compared to Johnny Cash." Tom Waits: "When Johnny Cash comes on the radio, no one changes the station."

Ah, there's the rub. When is the last time you heard a Johnny Cash song on a country radio station? There's no room for him and his kind anymore. Instead, we get something called Dierks Bentley. Or Rascal Flats. Or Montgomery Gentry. Homogenized, generic, bland.

Don't get me wrong. Some of the new stuff is good. I'm not such a crank that I think old is always better than new. It's just that radio doesn't seem willing to keep the past alive.

I know that everything in show business is about image. Johnny Cash was no exception. The whole "Man in Black" thing was a carefully crafted image. But all you've got to do is listen to anything he recorded—from "I Walk the Line" in 1956 to "Hurt" in 2003—and you'll hear the substance behind the image. As Leonard Cohen said, "Even after the song is done you hear him. The generations will be listening."

So, here's where it stands. Some time in the near future I will walk into our family room where my daughter will be watching country music videos. Some hunk in a sleeveless T-shirt and skintight jeans will be singing something about a Tiki bar. At first, I'll bite my tongue. But I won't be able to resist. I'll make the Old Geezer comment about how nobody ever plays Johnny Cash . . . or Merle Haggard . . . or Buck Owens . . . or Loretta Lynn anymore. I'll get the "Oh, Dad!" look, and then I'll shut up.

On second thought, maybe I won't shut up. After all, I'm a teacher. It's my job to educate the young. They need to know about the Mona Lisa, about Shakespeare, and about Johnny Cash, the Man in Black.

THE SWEET SCIENCE

I should have turned the TV off. But I didn't. Instead I just sat there, mesmerized.

The year was 1982, a cold, gray Saturday afternoon in November. I'd finished grading papers and didn't have anything better to do. Ray "Boom Boom" Mancini was fighting a Korean boxer named Duk Koo Kim at Caesar's Palace, and so I watched.

It was not a pretty fight. No fight with Mancini was ever pretty because he cut so easily. He usually won, but afterwards his doughy face always looked as though it had been run through a meat grinder.

Pretty or not, the fight thrilled. For thirteen rounds a bloodied Mancini pummeled his opponent and got pummeled in return. Both fighters, though small, pounded each other with blows that might have leveled a heavyweight. In the later rounds Kim suffered terrific punishment, and I remember thinking, "How much more can he take?" I silently wished he would just go ahead and fall.

Toward the end, with Mancini hitting him almost

at will, Kim staggered to the right side of the ring but still didn't go down. The announcer mentioned, rather matter-of-factly, that in a press conference before the fight the Korean kid had vowed to win the title or "die trying."

Then, it happened.

A vicious, compact hook from Mancini in the fourteenth round hit Kim flush on the temple. He crumpled and dropped to the canvas. I thought to myself, "That's it. He won't get up now." Less than a week later, Duk Koo Kim died in a Nevada hospital.

Seeing a man killed in the ring should have put me off the sport for good. Certainly, that fight made continuing as a boxing fan hard to justify. But vicarious violence is addictive; and so I still watched, occasionally, though never again in quite the same way. Boxing is a guilty pleasure. After this fight, watching yielded far more guilt than pleasure.

As a kid, I'd read and heard stories about the great fighters of the '30s, '40s, and '50s: Jack Dempsey, Gene Tunney, Joe Louis, Rocky Marciano, Jersey Joe Walcott and the like. But they were mostly just names. I knew bits and pieces of their larger than life history and had seen a few of their pictures in books. But I didn't quite know what they were about.

I didn't really become a boxing fan until 1971, when ABC's *Wide World of Sports* held a tournament of sorts aimed at choosing a worthy opponent for the former champ, Muhammad Ali. As every student of boxing history knows, Ali had been stripped of his title a few years earlier, at the zenith of his career, for resisting the draft and refusing to go to Vietnam ("Man, I ain't got nothing against them Viet Cong," he'd said).

Deep down I knew Ali was the legitimate champ, but I didn't want to admit it. I couldn't stand his loud-mouth antics, his braggadocio, his cocksure arrogance. It wasn't until later that I'd come to regard him as he regarded himself, "The Greatest."

At any rate, I watched week after week as fighters beat each other up for the future privilege of climbing into the ring with Ali and earning a huge payday.

For a while it looked as though the aging Floyd Patterson would be the one. But Patterson lost to Jimmy Ellis. Then Jerry Quarry, tagged by bigots and racists as "The Great White Hope," had a brief chance. Eventually, Joe Frazier won out.

Much to my delight, Smokin' Joe won his first bout with Ali to take the heavyweight crown. But two years later as I sat with my brother on the top bunk late at night, my ear pressed against a transistor radio, listening incredulously through the static, Frazier lost his title to a hulking young fighter named George Foreman. Unbelievably, young George knocked the champ down six times in two rounds before the referee stopped the carnage. Pictures in the next week's *Sports Illustrated* showed Foreman's vicious uppercuts actually lifting the smaller Frazier off the canvas.

For a couple of years in the early '80s I avidly followed the career of Sugar Ray Leonard. I didn't like him—another pretty boy like Ali—but he was undeniably good.

Then came the Mancini fight, forcing boxing fans everywhere to confront the ugly truth: that boxing is the rawest, most primal of all sports. You probably shouldn't watch; but once drawn in, it's hard to turn away.

WHITE ELEPHANTS

I like my house. It's comfortably cluttered. It's got that "lived-in" look because it's been, you know, lived in. When we built it almost a decade ago, my wife and I worried that it felt so blank and impersonal. It didn't take us long to solve that problem. Dozens of full bookshelves, lots of kids' artwork, framed family photos, and my wife's beautiful handcrafted quilts have truly made our house a home.

Occasionally, however, I get the urge to hang a set of dentures on the door frame.

You heard right. When I was a kid, my next-door neighbor's upstairs den had a pair of false teeth screwed shoulder-high to the wall, just inside the door. I'm pretty sure they were a kind of strange bottle opener, though I never really saw them used as such.

It was a bit disconcerting to walk in and see a full set of teeth, gums and all, grinning at you. Not the kind of thing you'd typically see in *Better Homes and Gardens*. Still, the dentures-on-the-wall helped make the room unique, gave it its own Addam's

Family personality.

Here's another white elephant you'll never see in *House Beautiful*: a turquoise high-heeled shoe, made of alligator-skin, filled with concrete and used as a doorstop. My great Aunt Booty had such a thing, and, to be honest, I always thought it rather elegant. I guess I should know better now that I'm older and more sophisticated.

(Technically, a true white elephant must be one-of-a-kind, so Aunt Booty's doorstop doesn't really qualify. Aunt Myrtle had one just like it.)

I'm a big fan of such stuff. I like oddities, things that don't quite fit. Conversely, I hate a room that's too perfect, where you're scared to sit on the furniture and where everything's been decorated to within an inch of its life. I want a room where, if you feel like it, you can kick your shoes off, prop your feet up on the table and have a chat with the cigar-store Indian standing in the corner.

As a teacher, I've come to realize that the profession demands a well-honed sense of "white elephant-ism." Grade-school teachers understand this best. Their classrooms teem with offbeat stuff, all kinds of gadgets and gizmos: gyroscopes and kaleidoscopes, snake skins and seashells, giant books and alphabet people, seeds sprouting from paper cups, cocoons morphing into butterflies, hamsters, ant farms, bells, maracas, xylophones and tambourines. Bits of this and pieces of that. Anything to make a kid wonder.

At the other end of the spectrum, college professors usually eschew such props. They teach in generic classrooms, bland spaces assigned to them for a semester, with little to indicate whether the course is in history or philosophy, mathematics or literature. The professor's talent lies in using words alone to bring ideas to life.

My own classroom—a huge open loft at the top of an old three-story building—contains a menagerie of quirky artifacts. A few are actually teaching aids, but most are just oddities—things too strange to keep at home but too unusual to let go of. They function mainly as conversation pieces, things to spark questions and comments from my sophomores and seniors ("So, Mr. Amos, why do you have that life-size chicken-wire man hanging from your ceiling?")

Some of my really good classroom stuff includes:

A fragment of eighteenth century red brick, imprinted with a cat's paw (I've often wondered whether eighteenth century cats looked like modern ones, or have cats changed as much as people have?)

A marvelously realistic plaster-cast lamp of The Incredible Hulk (a "gift" from a friend whose wife didn't want it in their house. Hard to believe, eh?). He's missing both his hands, due to an accidental bump from a clumsy student several years ago. Still, I keep him as a reminder not to lose my temper, as I've been known to "Hulk Out" on occasion.

A Zebra putter and some golf balls for practicing before school (My classroom floor breaks sharply to the left). To strengthen their concentration, I occasionally make students putt and recite poetry simultaneously.

Add to these a terra cotta bust of Elmer Fudd, a troupe of literary finger puppets, jars of Cape Hatteras pebbles, a jointed Shakespeare action figure (armed with a plastic quill), a peculiar assortment of posters, maps and books, and you get a sense of where I do my work.

All I'm really missing is a good set of false teeth.

Ain't Bobby So Cool

My children are starting to get suspicious. For years I've been telling them that Bob Dylan is their eccentric uncle who never comes to visit. I've slipped a few pictures of him into the family photo albums, and I've even assured them that one day their famous songwriting uncle will take a break from touring and drop by the house for dinner.

But the older they get, the harder they are to fool. The fact that Bob continues to be a no-show at family gatherings has begun to raise questions. My kids are pretty sharp. I think they suspect the truth. But they're also really kind, so it's possible they just keep playing along because they understand the old troubadour's importance to their dad.

I first got hooked on Bob Dylan as a sophomore in high school, when one day my friend Gub brought a copy of *Blonde on Blonde* to algebra class. She tossed it to me and said, "Here, I hate this stuff, but you might like it." I've felt indebted to her ever since.

The weirdly nasal voice, the brash harmonica, and

the jangling electric guitars captured me completely. And the lyrics? Those wild, rambling things, ranging from the ethereal to the philosophic, from the surreal to the outrageously comic? I loved the whole crazy package.

I even loved the cover, a full-length shot of Dylan strolling down the streets of New York in a pea jacket, wearing the most caustic, world-weary sneer I'd ever seen. For the rest of my time in high school I tried to imitate that sneer. I never managed to look like Dylan—nose not hooked enough—but I sure tried to cultivate the attitude and the persona. In every yearbook shot of me from then on, I'm attempting the cool, detached Dylan scowl.

It sounds funny now, but nothing could have been more serious then. For me Bob Dylan was poet, prophet, and cynical observer. He was the artistic witch doctor, who (as he said in a recent interview) had made a deal with "the big chief commander." He was Rebel Jester and Spiritual Riddler all rolled into one.

When Dylan sang about "visions of Johanna" or "the dancing child with his Chinese suit" or the bricks on "Grand Street, where the neon madmen climb," I had no idea what he was talking about. But it didn't matter. Cool was cool. How could a future English teacher resist such a wordsmith?

After Gub's gift I started collecting all of Dylan's old stuff: early acoustic folk records full of classic protest songs. Mid-'60s albums with all of their psychedelic symbolism. And the late-decade Nashville recordings that eventually would inspire the whole country-rock movement.

But even as I was collecting the old, he continued to produce the new. Inspired records like *Blood on the Tracks* helped get me through high school. His Christian albums in the early '80s opened my ears to gospel music. Whatever he sang, I listened.

For more than forty years now, Dylan's done the unexpected. He's not like those sad old rockers that go on "reunion" tours, recycling their hits for adoring audiences in order to make a quick buck. Dylan, love him or hate him, really does defy categorization.

In the last five years alone he has: played his music before the pope, starred in a Victoria's Secret commercial, won a Grammy and an Oscar, been nominated for a Nobel Prize in literature (the first songwriter ever considered), written and starred in his own movie, and published a critically acclaimed memoir. All this in addition to a couple new albums and several hundred concert dates. Not bad for an old buster.

Not long ago I took my younger daughter to a Bob Dylan/Willie Nelson concert. Her initial response was, "That's a whole lot of ugly on one stage." Ugly it was, but also really, really cool. Two absolutely American originals doing their thing.

Soon both my girls will start bringing their boyfriends home to meet the parents. I'm warning them right now: all potential fiancés had better be open-minded about Bob Dylan. I won't insist that they be fans, but they'd better at least be willing to listen. After all, family is family, and even a crazy uncle deserves a little respect.

Hunting the White Whale

Some pictures from childhood stay with you: a portrait of John the Baptist's head on a platter, staring glassy-eyed from the pages of the family Bible; a calendar of cute babies from the Gerber Company, tacked to the closet door in my grandmother's spare bedroom; a framed painting of dogs smoking cigars and playing poker, hanging on the wall of a rented beach house.

But no image sticks with me more vividly than the last page of a kids' version of *Moby Dick* I once saw at my cousin's house. It was a slick, oversized picture book with a front cover of a sailor keeping lookout from high up in the crow's nest.

Of course, this was just a kid's book, but it proved an early introduction to something much huger, much more mysterious and potent. At the time I didn't know about the real thing. I certainly didn't know that Herman Melville's epic novel about the monomaniacal Captain Ahab contained 135 chapters and weighed in at more than 500 pages.

Nor did I know that the book, when first published, had failed miserably, selling fewer than 1,000 copies of its original printing. Or that the author had died a broken and forgotten man, unaware that his master-work would one day be regarded by some as the greatest novel ever written.

No, I was oblivious to all that. I came to the story through the pictures. And to a kid's eye, they were pictures of captivating power. Especially the final page.

There stands Ahab perched upon the wrinkled back of the white whale, amid the swirl of the sea, trying to balance himself on a peg-leg carved of whalebone. His grizzled hair and Quaker beard blow madly in the wind. Though ensnared in a web of harpoon lines, he's stabbing crazily with his lance at the beast who had taken his leg so many years before.

He's trying to kill the unkillable, to fathom the unfathomable, to penetrate the impenetrable. One look at that picture and, even as a child, I understood obsession.

As an adult I've read *Moby Dick* (the real thing) three times. It's one of the few books I'm willing to read and reread. Every five years or so, I take it off the shelf and plunge in. Like *The Iliad, The Odyssey, Paradise Lost*, or *The Bible*, *Moby Dick* is one of those works you never really finish. Even when you reach the last page, you know you'll be back some day.

And like any truly great work of literature, you'd better not read it unless you're prepared to be disturbed. Melville tackles all the big philosophical questions about life and God and the nature of the human heart. Sometimes his answers are shockingly, brutally blunt.

I still remember falling into a bit of a depressive funk the first time I read *Moby Dick*. The book put me down in an emotional hole. It was dark down there.

You can't read Melville's chapter on "The Whiteness of the Whale" without thinking that The Eternal may, in fact, be malignant. You can't read his description of sharks ravenously feeding on a whale corpse, or Mr. Stubb similarly feeding on a supper of whale steak—cooked rare—without considering that lust for blood is down deep in the nature of things.

Yet in spite of its darkness the book is also quite funny, mainly because of its narrator. You don't mind journeying into the dark with someone like Ishmael. He's a witty evangelist with regard to all things concerning whales. He's sarcastic and ironic without being bitter. He's savvy and shrewd, a deep philosopher for the common man. He's naïve at times, human always. He makes you smile, even as you're plumbing the blackest of truths.

The pictures in that old kids' book have remained with me for the better part of a lifetime, almost against my will: the harpooner Queequeg, tattooed from head to foot, kneeling in prayer before his wooden god Tojo; Ahab hammering a Spanish doubloon into the mast of *The Pequod* as reward for the first sighting of Moby Dick; Ishmael floating to safety on a coffin after the white whale has split the ship to shivers.

These illustrations hooked me early and eventually pushed—or pulled—me toward the real thing. And as we all know, The Real Thing can be dangerous.

Better watch what you leave within reach of the children.

JACK

Words fail me. A writer is supposed to be able to describe anything, but this is just too difficult. I simply don't have the ability to convey how perfectly Jack Barber played Santa Claus when I was a child.

In truth, Jack really didn't play Santa. He was Santa.

Get out of your mind the image of the bell-ringing characters at shopping malls. Forget the fake, cotton-candy beards and the pillow-stuffed bellies. Forget the patent leather boots and the painted red cheeks and the insincere jollity. After you've known the real thing, that other stuff is false as dicer's oaths.

Jack's Santa was elfish, sprightly, and just a little mysterious. When he dropped by the house on Christmas Eve, you knew that you'd just encountered magic. Even today's most cynical, most media-savvy children would have believed in this Santa. How could they not? He was it: The genuine article, the thing itself.

It's one thing to play Santa Claus in December, but Jack was Santa always. And not in some goody-goody, smarmy way. There was nothing sugary about

Jack Barber. As he strolled up Main Street on a hot August afternoon, wearing his dungarees and work shirt, his pipe clenched between his teeth, you strangely caught yourself thinking, "Hmm, there goes Santa Claus."

He wasn't an especially big man, not really round at all. And though he sported a beard and wire-rimmed spectacles throughout the year, they weren't what left the lasting impression. He just was Santa Claus, to the core. There's no other way to put it. I'm almost fifty years old, and I still believe because I knew the man.

I write so that I won't forget. My relationship with Jack Barber goes way back, and well beyond his role as St. Nick. Though he died many years ago, there are images of him I don't want to lose.

Bear Creek Lake: We are camping. My parents don't like to camp and so Jack has invited me to tag along with him and his family. It's 6:00 A.M. I'm lying in a sleeping bag, shivering from the cold. I hear whistling outside the tent and poke my head through the zippered opening. Santa Claus stands over a campfire, scrambling eggs in a cast-iron skillet, puffing on a pipe. I'm not a big fan of scrambled eggs, but I eat these. And they're good, though I'm not sure if the black flecks are pepper or pipe ash.

The Orange Review: Jack has hired half a dozen teenage boys to do odd jobs around the print shop on Wednesday evenings. He gives us all specific chores and then expects us to do them. If we perform well, he praises. If we don't, we are told in stern but fair language what we should have done. On rare occasions, after an especially egregious screw-up, we feel the full force of his displeasure, and one of us is fired, though the Santa Claus in him always rehires the culprit for the next week. In later years, I will realize that not all employers act with such openness and evenhandedness.

The Orange County Rescue Squad: Jack is as dedicated a squadsman as ever served Orange County. The siren sounds and he answers the call.

The Country Blasters: My father and uncle play harmonica in this jug band, but Jack is the percussionist. He plays a mean washboard.

White Oak Plantation: Jack has decided that town life is just too crowded. He's bought a piece of property out in the country and put up a one-room shack. He gives this haven from the hustle-and-bustle of Orange a grand name, "White Oak Plantation." Eventually, he will build a home and move his family here. But for now, he spends every weekend holed up in this tar-paper shack in the woods. I drop by for a visit, and Jack shows me around the property. The air is thick with mosquitoes, so he wears a rag soaked in citronella under his hat. He's happy.

I know that most people use the word "peculiar" as an insult. "So-and-so's kind of peculiar," they say, turning up their noses. It's their backhanded way of calling someone odd, or eccentric, or maybe even hard to get along with.

I think differently. To me the word means original, individual, colorful, and above all, real.

By this definition, Jack Barber was as peculiar as the day is long.

Would that we all lived lives of such marvelous peculiarity.

Joyriding

L ike a bat outta hell. That's a fairly accurate description of how my grandmother drove a car.
Mrs. Mary Colvin—Grandmama Mary to me—never
owned a convertible; but if there were any justice in
the world, she would have. Behind the wheel of a sporty
convertible, her free spirit would have soared.

In a poignant eulogy at my grandmother's funeral
several years ago, one of my older cousins spoke fondly
of the wild rides she had taken with Grandmama down
the Tickle-Tummy Road. The rest of the grandchildren knew exactly what she meant. She was referring
to the Tanners Road, just across from the entrance to
Woodberry Forest School.

My grandmother would load as many grandkids
as she could fit into her pre-1950 black Ford, pull the
starter, and then go racing down the Tanners Road.
Whenever she came to one of the many San Francisco-
style hills, she'd intentionally speed up, causing our stom-
achs to rise and fall with what can only be described as
Happy Nausea. It was sort of poor man's roller coaster.

Years later, when my first child was only a few months old, on the way home from the babysitter one day I accidentally took a hill a bit too fast. Just then, from the car-seat behind me, I heard a delighted giggle. My daughter's first true laugh echoed her father's laughter three decades earlier as he'd careened down the Tanners Road in the back seat of his grandmother's car.

After some time, Grandmama retired the old Ford. It sat for years out back between the hen house and the pigpen, a broken but still-exciting toy for curious grandchildren.

She replaced it with a silver Chevrolet Impala. I don't remember any joyrides down the Tanners Road in this car, but I do recall a trip to the Gordonsville swimming pool one sweltering summer afternoon.

I suppose my grandmother never drove more than thirty or forty miles at one time in her entire life. And I feel safe in saying that she never drove on the Interstate. So a trip from Madison Mills to Gordonsville was for her a longish jaunt.

When we reached the Gordonsville traffic circle, she knew she needed to go left down Main Street. So she went left, immediately, against traffic, heading toward Main Street, ignoring the circle's requirement that you must first turn right and then follow the circle around. I'm pretty sure, from the wink she gave me as she hung a sharp left, that it wasn't accidental. With my grandmother counterintuitive rules didn't apply. Why go right when you needed to go left?

In her later years—now driving a 1970 black Pontiac—she stalled out on the railroad tracks. She'd been to the grocery store; and as she reached the May

Fray crossing, the old car stalled just as a train was approaching. According to witnesses, she scrambled out of the car, abandoning it on the tracks, but then went back to rescue her groceries. Luckily, a passerby noticed what was happening and pulled her quickly to safety. Seconds later the train knocked the car several hundred feet down the tracks.

Soon after that incident my uncle tried to talk to her about giving up her driver's license. He lectured her gently about safety, about how giving up the car was for her own good, and about how she needed to think of others on the road. I'm sure he offered up all the rational arguments that the younger generation uses on the old, who have reached that difficult stage when driving is no longer practicable. I wasn't there for the big driving powwow with my grandmother; but I can picture her listening patiently, nodding agreement, and then, when the lecture's over, winking slyly, absolutely intent on maintaining her right to drive.

Driving a car is the supreme form of independence. Just ask any teenager about to get a learner's permit. Just ask any working adult who's temporarily without wheels because the car's in the shop. Or just ask any senior citizen, afraid that the next little fender-bender is going to be the last straw that causes the insurance company to deem him too great a risk.

My last memories of my grandmother are sad ones. Confined to a wheel chair in a nursing home, a victim of multiple strokes, she was mostly unable to recognize or speak to visitors. I much prefer remembering her behind the wheel of a car, pedal-to-the-metal, roaring headlong down the Tanners Road.

Old School (Part 1)

A couple of years ago a friend gave me a hand-made picture frame as a Christmas gift. He's an accomplished craftsman, so I was a bit surprised when I opened the package and found this rather primitive looking wooden square. Puzzled, I thanked him politely and flipped over the frame. Then everything made sense. On the back, scrawled in black marker, was the following: MADE WITH MAPLE FLOORING FROM THE OLD BELLEVIEW SCHOOL.

Just last week I asked another friend to refinish an old cabinet-style radio that had belonged to my grandfather. For years it had stood in my office, collecting dust. On the verge of throwing it out, I decided at the last minute to see if it might be cleaned up. I really didn't expect much, but the results were stunning. Cracked varnish and dry-rotted fabric gave way to warm wood tones and dark maroon velvet. As I was loading it into the van, my friend said, "You know, the material I used to cover the speaker grill came from the stage curtains at the Old Belleview School."

Both of my friends had scavenged materials thrown away during the school's renovation into apartments a few years back. And both had given me deeply personal relics of my youth.

You see, I grew up on Belleview Avenue and spent a good chunk of every day just messing around the grounds of the old school. Though it's changed in recent years, I still know it. I know it the way a sailor knows the sea, the way a Frenchman knows French.

I learned to play tennis by swatting balls at the school wall, where I'd drawn an imaginary net with a piece of coal. I'd also drawn a catcher's mitt so that when I got tired of tennis, I could jump straight to baseball (I once threw a perfect game against the National League All-Stars, striking out Maury Wills, Johnny Bench, and Willie McCovey in succession).

A flagpole in the middle of the front yard where all the neighborhood kids played football made for interesting play-calling. "Run your man into the flagpole and then cut to the goal line." I once saw a kid take a simple handoff straight up the middle. Head down, he plowed smack into the flagpole and knocked himself out. Of course, if the flagpole didn't get you, the privet hedge along the sideline would. Get tackled into the hedge and chances were that you'd fall five feet below onto the sidewalk. Belleview football was rough.

The old school grounds had a thousand good spots for playing hide-and-seek. The coal cellar around back, the trash-burning incinerator, and the stairwells leading down to the changing rooms—they always smelled faintly of urine—all made for terrific hiding places. But none were as good as the rickety metal fire escape that snaked up the back of the three-story building. It was the most obvious place to hide—everyone knew to look there first—but it was also the most fun. Once found, you had nowhere to run; but the thrill of being so high in the air on such an unsteady contraption more than compensated.

On weekends every basketball player in town showed up on the blacktop. Older guys parked their cars, opened the doors, turned up the radios, and played hoops until dark. It was the one place in town that actually practiced integration. On the outdoor court, with wooden backboards and net-less rims, it didn't matter if you were black or white. All that mattered was that you could shoot and rebound.

A scene: *It's almost sundown. My mother calls out across the neighborhood that supper's ready. I'm hanging around the huge sycamore tree, peeling bark off the trunk and picking up "fuzz-balls." The shortest route home is a straight shot across the blacktop, but I hop on my bike and take the long way home: up Peliso in the opposite direction and then down the alley sidewalk between the school and the freestanding cafeteria (where Miss Lizzy once drove her car through the wall). Pop a wheelie off the ramp onto the baseball field; cut through the playground, spinning tires in the pea-gravel; race between the giant white columns and clatter down the front steps with no hands; then, sprint home.*

Both of my scavenging friends understand the power of symbols. They know that a scrap of wood or fabric can conjure up powerful memories. I'm glad to have such friends.

Old School (Part 2)

A friend recently told me that he'd never had an inspirational teacher. Not one. It almost made me want to cry. Twelve years of schooling, and not a single teacher had connected with him. Unfortunately, his case isn't unique. It's depressing to think that school has been so uninspiring for so many people.

Part of the problem is that our culture doesn't really value education. We pay lip service, but deep down we don't really care that much. If we did, we'd have students attend school year-round; we'd lengthen the school day and demand that ineffective teachers be replaced. These are hard things, and strong opposition—from teachers, administrators, parents and students—says much about how we regard school. The simple fact is: we say education is important, but we don't act that way.

I'm a teacher, and I sometimes feel surrounded by kids who have learned to hate school from adults who hated school themselves. For most people school is something to endure, not something to enjoy. Sadly, teachers are often the worst culprits. Over the years I've worked with many terrific people, but I've also worked with some who loathed school with all the intensity of the most recalcitrant and unmotivated students. I have sympathy but no tolerance for them: if you've lost the drive, the spark, the enjoyment, it's time to get out. There's no room in teaching for the halfhearted.

I've loved school all my life. And I've been blessed with many good teachers. I'm sure when I was sitting in their classes, they didn't suspect a future teacher in their midst; but I was watching and learning, not only about math, science, history and English, but about the profession of teaching itself.

The teachers I remember fondly—and there are many—had this in common: they all were serious about school. My middle school history teachers, my high school science teachers, and the college professors who introduced me to the great works of English literature all were missionaries with a burning message they had to pass along. They loved their subject so much that they needed to share it.

But the most profound influences on my education—and my life—came in elementary school. Grade-school teachers too often get overlooked. However, surely they make the biggest and deepest impressions.

Mrs. Bernice Preddy, Mrs. Maud Grimes, Mrs. Dorothy Roberts, and Mrs. Rae Carter were "old school." I'm talking really "old school," and I use the term with the utmost respect. For them school was business. You didn't horse around. You learned. And that was as it should be.

These women were as much mothers as teachers. They were kind, generous and even loving at times. But mostly they were serious. They didn't take their jobs lightly. Somehow their seriousness about school— their unspoken insistence that school was work and that work was good—rubbed off on me. They didn't put a great deal of stock in the idea that school should be fun. School was my job, they seemed to be saying, and I must do my job well.

I never wrote or called to thank them properly for starting me out on the right track. Yet these teachers formed my first impressions of what should happen in a classroom. I can't really hear their voices anymore, but I can still see their looks of approval and disapproval in my mind's eye. I'm quite sure that at least some of whatever goodness I possess is attributable to these teachers who demanded goodness, who rewarded goodness, and who wouldn't tolerate anything less than goodness.

Teaching, unfortunately, can be a haven for the sloppy. It's too easy for a teacher to go into a classroom and wing it. Even at good schools, people can get by with bad teaching. I'm not talking about sincere failure. I'm talking about laziness and shoddy preparation. Too many teachers hold themselves to too low a standard, and they get away with it because the system doesn't consistently demand excellence. Such teachers—it only takes a few—degrade and trivialize a profession I believe is nothing less than sacred.

No one's perfect. I know I've failed in the classroom on countless occasions. I've done and said the wrong thing more times than I care to admit. But I try never to let myself coast or take short cuts. I can't. My "old school" teachers taught me better that.

The Cat and the Garden Hose

I tell stories. Not professionally, mind you. I don't hire myself out for parties as the evening's entertainment. I'm just an habitual teller of tales. No matter the topic of conversation, my tendency is always to reply with a story.

Two minutes into any conversation and I'm thinking, "That reminds me of something that happened to me once." It's just the way my mind works. I think in stories.

Of course, all good storytellers are notorious liars. They're not interested in telling the truth in any factual, historically verifiable sense. The official storyteller motto is: "Never let the facts get in the way of a good story." I'm sure I have embellished my own stock of stories so much that I don't really know anymore if I've got the facts straight. But for good storytellers, the truth doesn't depend upon facts. They're interested in a kind of truth that goes deeper than mere facts.

Storytellers are also great manipulators. They are trying to get a certain emotional response from their audience. The best can take a set of events and twist them to make you laugh or cry or even do both at the same time.

Let's say I wanted to tell a story about a cat and a garden hose. I might tell a story something like this:

She died in December. But this story takes place in October, a couple of months before her death, at the height of her illness. Everyone knew she would die soon, and they were all making their mental arrangements to cope with that fact.

One afternoon, terribly worried about her, he came home from work and found a cat, obviously very ill, hiding in a nook under the back steps. For some reason, he decided that he needed to get the poor creature away from the house. He wasn't sure if it was diseased or if it posed some kind of threat to his family. All he knew was that suddenly it was crucial to get the cat away from his house.

At first, he tried poking at it with the long end of a broom. It refused to move, whimpering slightly, but staying in its corner. He grew more and more distraught, almost frantic, as he realized there was nothing he could do to dislodge the animal from under the steps. The more he poked it, the more it refused to budge, and the more worried he became that it was going to die right there in front of him.

He finally decided that the only way to rouse this cat was to shoot it with a garden hose. He pulled the hose from the corner of the house, turned on the water, and sprayed the cat. It struggled to its feet, hobbled into the front yard, and collapsed beside the car.

Later he took it to the animal shelter in a shoe box and had it put to sleep, but the shame and embarrassment of the episode haunted him for years. Why hadn't he just left the poor thing alone to die in peace?

In succeeding years he explained the incident to himself in the only way that seemed to make sense: that all dying was particularized for him in that cat. Somehow that pathetic creature under the back steps was showing him not only that things die, but also that he must watch them die.

For him the cat's dying was an intrusion. What had motivated him to spray it with the hose was simply the sheer inconvenience and intrusion its dying represented. He was making a statement with that hose: "Listen, go die somewhere else. Die if you have to, but don't die where I've got to watch and be aware."

Again, this all took place in October. Two months later he would witness a different death, and one of the accomplishments of his life would be that he did not push that dying away as some sort of inconvenience or intrusion. It would have been very easy to avoid being with her on her last day. He could have come up with many, many excuses. But he didn't, and he was glad. The End.

That's a pretty good story about a cat and a garden hose. Is it true? Sure it is. Is it factual? Who can say? And really, what difference does it make? What matters is that it's a good story trying to get at the real truth.

SUGAR 'N' SPICE

A young pregnant mother strolls down the cereal aisle, her husband at her side. It's Sunday. Each of them holds a little girl by the hand. The girls wear pink leggings and frilly dresses trimmed in lace. The older girl, about five, has a white bow in her hair. The toddler wears a purple hat—hats look good on her. They're a nice family, just stopping on their way home from church to pick up a few odds and ends.

Then it happens. A stranger approaches. She's an older woman, maybe sixty, also dressed in her Sunday best. She looks at the couple and smiles. She bends down and speaks to both girls, chucking them under the chin and talking baby talk. When she stands up again, she looks at the mother and says with a perfectly straight face, "Oh, you're pregnant. I'll bet you're hoping for a boy."

My wife and I suffered through that scenario a number of times way back when she was pregnant with our third child. Every time it happened it made me want to spit. No matter how you cut it, the unspoken assumption was that "girls are nice, but boys are better."

Part of my anger stemmed from the fact that these people would make their comments right in front of the girls, as though kids don't have ears to hear. It bugged me that anyone could look at two beautiful children and say something seemingly so ignorant and insensitive.

I always wanted to respond with sarcasm but never did. You know, something along the lines of, "Yeah, these two will do, but I won't really be happy until I father a man-child." Instead, I just bit my tongue.

That was a long time ago, and I've calmed down since. My reaction was probably an overreaction. People mean well. However, such comments—even if well intentioned—do reflect the subtle and not-so-subtle prejudices our society has about women and men. Many people of both sexes still operate on the assumption that men are boss, men win the bread, men have the brains, men wear the pants, and that no family is complete without a boy.

Most people today at least know they can't say this kind of thing out loud, but they still think it and act it.

A quick story:

For the first year of our marriage, my wife and I lived in a seedy little apartment across from the racetrack in Laurel, Maryland. Above us lived a couple who fought constantly. I'm not sure if they were married, but I assumed they weren't. On several occasions over the course of the year the man beat up his girlfriend. I know because the walls were thin. I can still hear the screams.

Lying in bed trying to go to sleep, we'd hear a dull

thud, followed by horrific, guttural, animal-like howls. "Stop it! Somebody please make him stop it! Will somebody please make him stop?"

The first few times it happened I called the police. I'd grown up with the old-fashioned notion that policemen could fix anything. I was sure that they would come and cart this monster away, and the poor woman upstairs would be saved. Not so.

The police were always sympathetic, but because the woman wouldn't press charges, their hands were tied. After a few minutes they'd just pack up and leave. Eventually I quit calling.

The few times I saw the man during daylight hours, he looked just like a regular guy, wearing jeans and a baseball cap. The girl too looked just like hundreds of others you see walking around every day. No cuts or bruises. Just a regular person. For certain, she was someone's daughter, maybe someone's sister.

Here's what I want: I want a world where my daughters can do what they choose, where they don't have to be submissive, and where they will be free from the threat of physical violence.

Though I'm probably spitting against the wind, I want a world with more "gentle men." This has nothing to do with chivalry. I'm not talking about knights in shining armor opening doors for ladies or putting women on a pedestal. And I'm not talking about men becoming sensitive and soft and sappy. I'm just talking about making the world a decent place for my girls and for every other father's girls.

True gentlemen are in short supply. We ought to cultivate more of them.

LORENE

One of my favorite books begins with the narrator getting killed in the first chapter. He then narrates the remainder of the novel from the afterlife. Waking up in the second chapter, the narrator finds himself neither in heaven nor hell, but in a sort of vast, cosmic movie theater with nine screens running simultaneously. As he watches, he realizes that these movies are really the stories of his ancestors' lives.

One screen is about his great-great grandfather who fought in the Revolution. One tells the story of another family patriarch, an eighteenth century Welsh minister. Gradually the narrator begins to understand that, during his life on earth, his own character and personality were deeply influenced by these people from his past—people he never even knew existed.

Years from now, when my own great-grandchildren are sitting in that big Theater in the Sky, I'm sure at least one screen will be devoted to my father's mother, Eva Lorene Amos.

How best to describe this woman, my grandmother,

without using words and phrases that would apply to anyone's grandmother? How about a list of "un's"?

Lorene Amos was: unsophisticated, uneducated in any formal sense, untraveled, and unwealthy. But she was also unpretentious, undaunted by a hard life, un-inhibited in her speech, unwilling to suffer fools, and unflinching in the face of the cancer that eventually killed her.

Some scenes from a life:

In church: It is dusk on a summer evening during annual Revival services at Lower Rapidan Baptist. The windows to the little stone church are open. Insects buzz around the yellow lights. Along with her brothers and sisters, she belts out the words to "Throw Out the Lifeline" and "Toiling On." Later, a bald-pated visiting evangelist in a blue-serge suit, preaching hellfire and damnation, shouts about the Spirit of God. To my young ears it sounds as if he's talking about the "Spit" of God. I'm tired, so I curl up on the pew, put my head in her lap, rub her thumb—it feels like the silk edge of a blanket—and fall asleep.

Doing laundry: She stands at the ironing board on the back porch of the cracker box house she and Granddaddy rent on Williams Drive. She's wearing a flowered sleeveless shift and flip-flops. Grandmama Amos "takes in" laundry, which means she does other people's washing and ironing for pay. She spreads a shirt on the board and sprinkles starch-water from what looks like an Ivory soap container with an aluminum sprinkler head. She sings a bit and talks a bit. She puts one shirt on a hanger and moves on to the next. Dozens of shirts and pants hang from a rack in the corner.

On Main Street: Still in her shift and flip-flops, she and Granddaddy sit in the front seat of the Falcon just outside May Rudasill Department Store (though what really interests her is who's going into the liquor store next door). I'm in the back, eating a hamburger from Crane's Hamburger House. It's Friday evening and we are people-watching. This is high entertainment and (I realize now) much more instructive than any formal course in psychology.

Drinking coffee: She pours just a bit of coffee into a cup and saucer (part of a set of red-rimmed grocery store promotional dishes), then fills the remainder of the cup with Carnation canned milk until it overflows into the saucer. Slurping ensues.

When Lorene Amos' life is replayed on the Big Screen, there will be these and a thousand other scenes: making redeye gravy; cracking fresh coconuts with a hammer and nail; negotiating with the Jewel Tea salesman; teasing grandchildren about the old man who, she swore, lived in the attic and rolled pumpkins across the floor at night; watching her "stories" on afternoon TV (*General Hospital* and *Dark Shadows*); dusting the whatnot shelf; taking out her false teeth to the delight of her grandchildren; spending summer evenings chatting with neighbors under the mimosa trees in the front yard.

I spent a good portion of my high school years at my grandmother's house. Without my knowing it, she helped form my way of thinking, my way of speaking, and my way of living. I wish my own children could have known her, but I guess they'll just have to wait for the movie.

SLAVES TO FASHION

I went to a concert the other night in Downtown Charlottesville with some friends from work. I wore my standard uniform: cuffed corduroys so old the cords have worn slick, a white buttoned-down-collar shirt, a windbreaker, and a pair of slip-on loafers.

One guy in the group dressed with a bit more flair. He showed up in black slacks, black shirt, black leather jacket, and black beret cocked at a rakish angle. I've never been able to understand how people get away with that kind of thing, but somehow this fellow carried it off. Some folks just have the knack; they ooze style. If ever I dared to don such a getup, I'd look like a French freight train.

What we wear speaks to who we are. Clothes really do make the man (and the woman, too). A banker friend of mine wears banker's clothes: starched shirts, wool slacks with razor-sharp creases, cufflinks, perfectly knotted tie, and carefully buffed wingtips. The essence of spit and polish, he's crisper at the end of the day than I am at the beginning. And his clothes reflect his personality: precise, controlled, business-like, and classy.

I, on the other hand, am wrinkled from the get-go. I wear a tie each day, but that's my only concession to formality. I teach with my sleeves rolled up, a symbolic gesture that says, "Let's get down to business." I don't even own a pair of hard-soled shoes. Besides, they're for administrators; real teachers wear soft soles.

For years, my only suit was one I inherited from a deceased great uncle; eventually the wide lapels came back in style. I simply can't imagine wearing clothes that don't crumple. Like Huck Finn, I need to "stretch and gap" occasionally.

For the most part, adults have settled on an image. We've figured out who we are and dress accordingly. Kids, on the other hand, are tremendously susceptible to fashion lunacy. They're looking for an identity, and their struggle is reflected in the clothes they choose to wear. More accurately, it's reflected in the clothes the culture pushes them to wear: girls in skintight hip-huggers and midriff tops, brandishing designer labels like weapons; boys in low-riding baggy pants and base-ball caps turned backwards, strutting around in space-age sneakers that cost more than a good used car. None of it can possibly be comfortable; and all of it looks, by any objective measure, foolish.

It has ever been so. Ducktails, high-waters with white socks, and cigarettes rolled up in shirtsleeves during the 1950s. Tie-dyes, Nehru jackets, and embroidered bellbottoms in the '60s. Leisure suits, moon boots, and disco shirts unbuttoned to the navel in the '70s. It's all part of the same phenomenon. Somebody somewhere establishes what's cool. Then everybody everywhere follows along.

Once John Wayne appeared in a movie wearing his belt off-center. It was purely by accident. No matter. For the next year off-center belts were all the rage. People who don't know who they are look to be told. Celebrities and fashion gurus gladly fill the void.

When I was a student at Orange County High School in the mid-'70s, Converse Chucks were the ultimate in swank footwear. I spent twelve hard-earned dollars on a pair of green high-tops. It didn't matter that their plain canvas uppers and flat rubber soles gave my weak ankles no support. If I'd had more money to blow, I'd have bought Chucks in black, white, red, blue, yellow, and purple, as well.

A big part of my joy at making the varsity basketball team as a sophomore was being issued a new pair of burnt-orange Chucks to go along with the rest of my uniform: short shorts, sleeveless jersey, and knee-high stockings striped orange and blue. We went 4-11 that season; but, man, we looked good.

There's a terrific old Robert Burns poem titled "To a Louse." It describes a fashionable lady sitting proudly in church, wearing her Sunday finery. Her hair is coiffed in the latest style, and clearly she wants to be seen. What she doesn't realize is that there's a louse crawling up the back of her neck. Burns ends the poem with this bit of Scottish wisdom: "O wad some Power the giftie gie us, to see oursels as ithers see us." A rough translation: "If only the gods would give us wisdom enough to see ourselves through the eyes of others."

If only. If only.

T. O.'s

They say that blood is thicker than water, but I'm here to tell you: It ain't necessarily so. That old saying is supposed to mean that family loyalty trumps everything, that nothing runs deeper than blood and kinship. But if that's true, how come I always preferred T. O.'s to Johnny Kube's?

Johnny Kube was my great-uncle, a tall, dignified—and often bow-tied—Virginia gentleman, who ran a small general store just past the entrance to Woodberry Forest School. He lived in the house next door, and every day he'd walk twenty yards from home to work, where he sold everything from clothing to canned goods.

Occasionally, my cousins and I would troop through the maze of cornfields that separated my grandmother's place from Kube's store. We'd buy a handful of penny candy and then head back down the road. It was just another way to pass the time after we'd exhausted all the other alternatives (like collecting hickory nuts, exploring the tool shed, and hiding out in the meat house).

Johnny Kube's tiny, white cinderblock store was torn down some time ago; but in its heyday, it was one of dozens of such stores that dotted the Virginia landscape. In fact, just two miles away, barely a stone's throw from the Rapidan River, stood T. O. Gillum's General Merchandise. Family or not, for me, Kube's just couldn't compare.

What could you buy at T. O's? My goodness, what couldn't you buy?

Let's start with food. On the canned-goods shelf behind the counter you could find: pork 'n' beans, deviled ham, Vienna sausages, soups and stews, peanut butter, jelly, and all sorts of vegetables. And if you were in the mood for something more exotic, you could always go with—my personal favorite—sardines in barbecue sauce.

Then there were the snacks: Nabs and animal crackers, pecan pinwheels and cream-filled oatmeal cookies, Fireballs and Mary Janes. And ice-cold drinks from the reach-down-in cooler: Chocola, grape Nehi, YooHoo, and cream soda, all in frosty glass bottles. What you couldn't get, of course, were expensive bottled waters or any of the frou-frou stuff sold in today's convenience stores.

T. O.'s was also a haberdashery of sorts. I bought my first pair of Red Camel bib-overalls there; and had I needed such items, I could have bought belts, socks, suspenders, shoes, hats, coats and bandanas. I could also have equipped myself with a corncob pipe, smoking tobacco, chewing tobacco, pocketknife, and fishing lures.

In addition to such a wide range of merchandise, T. O.'s was also a filling station and a post office. Where else could you pick up your mail and then have the postmaster pump your gas? His was truly a "general" store. He had what you needed; and if he didn't have it, you probably didn't need it.

But what really made the place special was the man himself. T. O. Gillum was no salesman. He was not a fast-talker. Yet he was a man of infinite, easy conversation. He treated everyone who walked through his doors as a friend, not as a customer. He asked about your family, and it was clear that he really wanted to know. He talked about local politics, about the national news, about the latest wreck on the wicked curve just in front of the store. (The only time I ever saw him at a loss for words was when I asked him to describe the day the chitterling truck overturned. He just smiled a bemused smile.)

But no matter where the conversation started, it eventually came around to baseball. He loved the game, and nobody knew more about it than T. O. In the days before ESPN, he got his sports information the old-fashioned way: he studied the box scores in *The Post* and could tell you just about anything you wanted to know, especially about the perennially awful Washington Senators. (We were both fans of slugger Frank Howard and "Steady" Eddie Brinkman, the Senators' all-glove, no stick shortstop).

When you stopped at T. O.'s, time didn't matter. It was perfectly possible to go in for a single item and come out an hour later. For many, the single-item errand was just an excuse to stop by for company and conversation.

Compare all this to the modern convenience store. Rush in, rush out. Pay at the pump. Order your lunch on a screen. No human interaction. We've sold our souls for a mess of pottage.

Actually, T. O. probably carried pottage. In a can, right there on the shelf next to the sardines.

PLUM

One function of wine is to cleanse the palate. I'm not a wine drinker, but I do understand the concept. Certain books can serve the same function.

My taste in literature tends toward the dark. My idea of a happy ending is the flood at the end of *The Grapes of Wrath,* where a young woman, who has recently lost her baby, bares her breast to nurse a starving old man back to health.

I enjoy books that delve deeply into the human condition, books that refuse to sugar over the difficulties of living. I appreciate the honesty of writers who don't flinch from showing pain and suffering in all its reality.

And yet, after a spate of such books, when I've almost convinced myself that life is "dull, nasty, brutish, and short," I pull down a copy of Wodehouse just to cleanse my palate.

The name's pronounced "Wood-house." P. G. Wodehouse. Pellham Greenville. Known to his friends simply as "Plum," he's best remembered as author of the Bertie and Jeeves stories. But he's also the guy who peopled his books with characters like Gussie Finknottle, Catsmeat Potter-Pirbright, the Honorable Galahad Threepwood, Stilton Cheesewright, and a raft of other good-natured nitwits every bit as silly as their names.

Wodehouse. Author of more than ninety novels and 300 short stories, all gently skewering the inanities of English aristocracy. The man who once wrote to critics who had complained that his most recent book was simply the same old plot with different characters: "I'll fix you. My next book will be the same old plot with the same old characters."

Wodehouse. The man about whom the *Washington Post* once wrote, "His world is the world of the well-born and the highly-placed, who say 'dash it' when troubles come and 'right ho' when they vanish." What better tonic for the student of overly serious literature than a good healthy shot of Wodehouse?

Every winter I teach Shakespeare's *Hamlet*. I love the play because it's dark and because it depresses me. To my mind, no other work of literature gets so truly at the way things really are.

But every time I teach it, the play begins to dominate my thinking in ways that aren't entirely healthy. I find myself during supper mulling over Hamlet's line, "A man may fish with a worm that hath eat of a king and eat of the fish that hath fed of the worm." I wake up thinking about phrases like "too, too sullied flesh," and "the quintessence of dust."

Once, while playing board games with my children, I got Hamlet's metaphor for childbirth stuck in my mind. It's nothing more, he says, than "the sun breeding maggots in a dead dog." Pretty bleak, depressing stuff. Bleak and depressing I can live with. Obsessive, unhealthy morbidity is something else entirely. Enter Wodehouse.

There are many comic writers, many humorists, many satirists and punsters. There is, however, only one Wodehouse. No other writer of English—other than Shakespeare, now that I think about it—revels quite so much in the sheer joy of playing with language. No other writer, other than Shakespeare in his comedies, takes such a generous view of the follies and flaws of silly human beings. No other writer, including Shakespeare, could ever have written the line—about Lord Emsworth making his daily trip to the pigsty to see his prize sow, the Empress of Blandings—"He pottered off pigward."

Every year, as a way of restoring my mind to health, I follow my teaching of *Hamlet* by reading a Wodehouse novel. It doesn't matter which one because they all follow the same pattern: things go haywire, and then things work out. The point of reading him isn't to think or analyze. It's simply to laugh at the foolishness, to marvel at the language, and to smile at the happy resolution. Wodehouse novels always, always end happily.

For me Wodehouse is more than just an escape. He's more than comic relief. Reading him is not just a way of denying the truths of *Hamlet*. I know Tragedy is true. But no more so than Comedy. Hamlet is right when he says the world is terrible. Life really is short.

We are just flesh, and we must suffer the slings and arrows of outrageous fortune. Dash it!

But Wodehouse is right also. Things work out. Life's not so bad. In fact, how bad can it be with Wodehouse to pick you up? Right ho!

BESIDE THE STILL WATERS

The 8:00 A.M. services are the simplest. A handful of worshipers. A church so quiet you can hear the floorboards creak. No choir. No hymns. Just a few readings and a short homily, followed by Holy Communion. That's it. Basic, unadorned, yet profoundly restorative.

I like the quiet. After a hectic week, it's good just to sit. Sometimes I think; sometimes I pray. Sometimes I simply am.

Always I look at the window. A woman in a long robe stands on the rocks at the edge of a quiet stream. She's holding a dove in her hands. Maybe she's comforting it. Maybe she's about to release it. Either way, the bird doesn't struggle. Purple mountains rise in the background.

Nothing moves, and yet the stained-glass scene is not static. Rather, it's a living serenity, a breathing calm. At the bottom of the window reads a familiar caption from David's Twenty-third Psalm: BESIDE THE STILL WATERS.

The woman by the stream is only one in a series of beautiful stained-glass windows at St. Thomas' Episcopal Church on Caroline Street in Orange.

I sit in the same pew each Sunday.

Immediately to my left, Jesus knocks at a large wooden door; he's holding a lantern that seems to glow even when the church is dark.

In the window directly opposite a knight kneels, sword in hand, ready to receive Christ's blessing (I always picture St. George setting out to slay the dragon). One window shows a group of Roman soldiers lying prostrate, stunned by the risen Christ and the empty tomb. In another, the Master instructs a group of young children gathered at his feet.

Most visitors, however, are drawn to the Tiffany original in the front left corner, where a tall, stately angel in flowing gown announces, BLESSED ARE THE PURE IN HEART, FOR THEY SHALL SEE GOD.

These windows startle. You don't expect to see such art in a small-town church. Yet there they are. They humble. They awe and inspire. None more so than the serene woman beside the quiet stream with a dove in her hands.

A friend of mine, a Presbyterian minister no less, insists that "the Episcopalians have got it right. They've got stuff for you to look at during church when your mind begins to wander."

I'm not sure I'd put it that bluntly, but I know what he means.

Most Protestant churches eliminated the decorations a long time ago. After all, the Puritans weren't called Puritans for nothing. They felt a need to purify the Catholic Church, which in their view had gone too far in its ornamentation. They worried that people in the pews might actually start worshipping the images and icons instead of God himself.

My sense is that they threw the baby out with the bathwater.

They gutted the service of liturgy and ritual, of symbol and beauty. And they replaced it with instruction and sermonizing. So if you don't like long sermons—and I don't—blame them on the Puritans.

Much as I love the windows at St. Thomas', I'm sure I don't "worship" them. They're simply tools to get my mind and spirit moving in the right direction. They help me focus.

I need them, just as I need the Alpha and Omega symbols on the altar. Just as I need the changing colors on the priest's stole, the rhythms of the church calendar, the ritual response to prayers, and all the other liturgical aids to worship.

I realize this puts me in a pretty serious minority. Most people today prefer the casual. It's no coincidence that the fastest growing churches in America are the ones that stress freedom and spontaneity over tradition and ritual. Many people simply don't see the value in all of that stiff, formal nonsense. Most think that ritual just gets in the way. They see it as a hindrance, not a help.

I think otherwise. I crave the permanent, the unchanging. I like doing the same thing, over and over.

And so I sit, each Sunday, under the placid gaze of the woman by the stream.

There's a reason they call this place a "sanctuary."

It's a retreat from the rattle and hullabaloo of a world gone wrong. Here schedules and obligations fade away. Here headlines and worries, fears, frettings and failings disappear, if only for a time.

It's the one place left where I can sit and be still, "beside the still waters."

If Winter Comes

Evening comes early these days. Daylight fades fast. The time just changed. Better cram it in now, while we can.

A breeze blows brisk. The mountains in the distance shift between blue and purple as cloud-shadows scud across an early fall sky. Overripe persimmons litter the ground, their winy, rotten-sweetness attracting swarms of buzzing yellow jackets. The majestic oak stands proudly beside the creek, almost bare. A carpet of bronze needles encircles each white pine. Maple leaves, red and orange, swirl in funnels across the ground, like miniature twisters. The geese left weeks ago, almost unnoticed.

It's November on the golf course, and I'm just a little bit sad.

November is when even the tough guys get wistful. Just the other day my partner let slip a moving little comment that caught perfectly the bittersweet aura of a golf course in fall. Between cussings, he said: "Playing this time of year is both happy and sad. The days are so short. You know it's coming to an end, but everything is so beautiful. I know it sounds weird, but it makes me think of my grandmother. When she died, we were sad; but at the same time we knew she was all right." The macho act disappears for just a moment as thoughts of mortality obtrude.

Golfing on this late afternoon in early November, we're trying to squeeze the last drop of juice from the orange.

Soon winter will arrive, and we'll be at the mercy of the weather. We'll try to sneak in a few holes after work, but darkness falls too soon. We'll pull out the long-johns and stocking caps and try to convince ourselves that 32 Fahrenheit is "not too cold, as long as the wind's not blowing."

We'll carp about the unfairness of hitting a good shot onto a frozen green and watching the ball bounce sky-high, as though it's just landed on a sidewalk. We'll invoke "the leaf rule," an unwritten agreement among wintertime golfers that balls lost in the leaves will not incur a penalty.

Some will winterize their carts with zippered plastic covers and propane heaters. Those of us without such accessories tell ourselves that walking is "good for us; we should do more of it."

We're all dreading the inevitable. Soon there will be snow. And we all know what that means.

With snow on the ground we're reduced to haunting the golf shops—quick Saturday trips to the city just so we can moon over the latest equipment and jaw with all the other sad junkies looking for a wintertime fix. Back home, we'll reread all the old golfing magazines, daydreaming over the glossy photos of swanky courses we know we'll never play. If we get really desperate, we'll cook up a fantasy golf vacation on the Internet.

When the snow finally begins to melt, at the first sign of grass peeping out from blankets of white, we'll head to the range and beat balls. The course won't be playable, but the range will have thawed enough that we can swing a little. In a few days, we hope, barring another snowstorm, we might get to play a few holes, at least the ones without too much shade.

We love Central Virginia, but this time of year we wish we lived just a little farther south. We wonder what the weather's like in Williamsburg? Whether it snowed down in the Carolinas?

A few of us—the really tough ones—will meet on New Year's Day, no matter the weather. A little sleet? So what? We've checked the Weather Channel and found "about a two-hour window" when the temperature will rise and the rain will ease up. As the sleet freezes on our caps and the ice water runs down our backs, as the club slips in our hands and our shoes begin to leak, we'll bellyache about how the weather forecasters "never get it right."

Real golfers love the game with a passion that sometimes defies reason. The game's hold on us doesn't disappear just because the seasons change. Golfers live on a kind of faith that the rest of the world would do well to emulate. We don't hibernate. We percolate. We dream. We hope.

We know, deep down, that the poet's words are true: "If winter comes, can spring be far behind?"

The Town Council

You won't catch these guys sipping lattes in the morning. In fact, most of them wouldn't know a latte if it jumped up and bit them on the behind. No, they're coffee drinkers, plain and simple.

I'm talking about the McDonald's crowd, a bunch of good-natured local geezers who gather each morning to solve the world's problems over their daily cup of joe.

There are two kinds of coffee drinkers and two kinds of shops that cater to them. First, you've got your coffee snobs. ("Afficionados" may be a more polite term.) They need variety and choice. Some days they want "Organic Raspberry Burst" and other days only "Marshmallow Pecan Truffle" will do. They don't think twice about forking over $3.50 for a White Mocha Grande.

For these folks, selection matters, and so does atmosphere. Drinking coffee is an "experience." They need a place with china mugs, stuffed chairs, and a guitar in the corner, preferably one strummed by a beatnik in a black beret. They need Internet access.

A student of mine recently took a job at one such upscale coffee bar. Before she began working, she took classes where they made her memorize all the varieties of coffee available and all possible permutations for mixing them. Sort of like being a nonalcoholic bartender.

At the other extreme, you have the indiscriminate crowd, who really don't give a hoot what the stuff tastes like. As long as it's hot, black, and comes in a Styrofoam cup, they're happy. They'll pay their thirty-nine cents (with senior discount), but only if it comes with free refills. Three dollars for a cup of java strikes them as slightly obscene.

These guys—it's strictly a guy-crowd—create their own atmosphere. Each morning around 8:00 the McDonald's dining room undergoes a miraculous transformation. The burger-flippers gradually fade into the background. The steel counter with its bank of cash registers melts away. Almost imperceptibly, the place becomes a country store, circa 1950.

This is where friends gather to share news, tell jokes, air complaints, and generally reminisce about times gone by. All that's missing is a potbellied stove. Though if you look closely, you can actually see one of those too, in your mind's eye.

I don't count myself among the coffee snobs, but I do enjoy drinking the good stuff on occasion. And I'm willing to pay a higher price for doing so. I'll even admit to an occasional latte. I like slurping the froth.

If I want to do a little breakfast reading, there's nothing like the ambiance of a swank coffee shop.

But I know it's not the real thing.

The real thing happens at Macdonald's.

The McDonald's crowd acts as an unelected, but nevertheless ultimately wise, "Town Council." Every morning they hash over the ins-and-outs of local politics: which ordinances don't make sense; which regulations are too intrusive; which properties are being bought, which sold, and for what purpose.

When they've exhausted this topic, they move on to the national scene. Then to sports and religion, the stock market and public education, television, women and whatever else strikes their fancy. All of it is larded with wit, sarcasm and a healthy dose of "can-you-believe-it" skepticism.

Sometimes they've got their facts straight, sometimes they don't; but it hardly matters, because the subtext of all their jawing is this undeniable truth: Times have changed, and not necessarily for the better.

These men recall simpler times: when children respected their elders, when teachers disciplined students, when the courts dispensed justice, when houses were built to last, when cars had real engines, when athletes played for the love of the game, when doctors made house calls, when movies weren't rated, when grocers made deliveries, when you could walk into a bank and get a loan that very day, when grades weren't inflated, and when "self-esteem" wasn't the end-all of education.

Though they'd never put it in such terms, these men are pining for a time when people understood the concept of community in their gut. They're guarding the citadel as the barbarians clamor at the gate.

Their little morning get-together is just a way of maintaining the tie that binds.

I suppose the work of a true Town Council ought to take place somewhere more "official" than a fast food joint, the very symbol of our modern obsession with impersonal speed and mass-production.

On the other hand, I like the irony. It's taking the battle straight to the enemy.

Bread: The Staff of Life

M an does not live by bread alone.

But teenaged boys do.

Here's the ritual that takes place in my kitchen every Saturday morning: My sixteen-year-old son stumbles out of bed, rubs the sleep from his eyes, and heads to the fridge. He grabs a can of Pillsbury Crescent Rolls, cracks it open on the edge of the counter, and then arranges the dough meticulously on a baking sheet. He preheats the oven, pops the pan onto the top rack, and waits till they're done. He's quite particular about these faux croissants and takes great pride in baking them to perfect doneness. It's an art, he insists, to getting them just crisp enough without being too doughy on the inside.

He's a polite kid, so he always offers me a couple, though I know he could eat the entire batch by himself. In fact, I'm sure he could down several dozen without breaking a sweat.

I know I could when I was his age.

I've always been a bread lover. My grandmother

used to make scads of homemade rolls just for me when she knew I'd be visiting. My mother, a teacher's aide at the high school, frequently brought home bags of Parkerhouse rolls she'd purchased from the cafeteria ladies. And though I was a brown-bagger myself, I made exceptions on days when the cafeteria served rolls. I'd suffer through the long line, turning up my nose at the Jell-O and fish sticks, just so I could get a plate—sometimes two—of dinner rolls. Nothing else. No meat. No vegetables. Just bread.

As an adult, I've taught myself how to cook. And though I'm no gourmet, I'm not bad. I can do entrees and side dishes, soups and stews, cakes and pies, pretty much the whole gamut. But my specialty is bread.

I love the yeasty odor of dough rising. I love the aroma of bread in the oven. It's the smell of home.

I've got dozens of recipes for bread of all kinds: corn bread and banana bread; spoon bread and foccacia; wheat bread, French braids, sourdough, olive bread, and baguettes. I've even experimented with challah, a Jewish holiday loaf. I do all manner of biscuits (I don't necessarily approve of Pillsbury prefabs, but since my son likes them, I make the concession).

I've gotten so good at certain breads that I don't even need a recipe: I could make corn bread in a cast iron skillet with my eyes closed, and Grandmama's angel biscuits in my sleep.

As with most things, simple is best. What follows is the finest, yet simplest, bread recipe I know.

5 c. all-purpose flour
1 t. salt
1 T. sugar

2 T. (or 2 packages) yeast

2 c. hot water

Combine all dry ingredients (including yeast). Add water and mix. Knead dough, adding a little flour if necessary. Place in greased bowl and let rise until doubled. Punch down dough. Divide and form into two round balls. Place on greased cookie sheet. Score loaves with a sharp knife. Dust with flour. Let rise until doubled. Bake at 400 degrees until done (20 minutes or so).

This bread, as a friend of mine says about any food of exceptional quality, is "table-grade."

I've used the recipe hundreds of times over the years. It's fed my family. It also has provided me with excellent mental therapy. Nothing dissipates anger, soothes sorrow, or calms worry better than kneading bread dough.

That's why I've never understood the appeal of bread machines. In baking bread, the process matters at least as much as the product; and bread machines completely negate the process. Convenient? Yes. Tasty? Maybe. True Bread? No way.

There's nothing therapeutic about dumping a bunch of ingredients into a machine and flipping a switch. And there's nothing beautiful about a loaf of bread that comes out looking like a giant coffee can with a hole in the middle.

Really good bread is more than mere food. Really good bread feeds not just the body, but the soul. It's communion. It's manna from heaven. It—and a few fishes—can miraculously feed a multitude.

So go on. Bake some bread. All it takes is a little time, a little effort, a little patience, and a little love.

Haute Cuisine

I always expected the Blue Plate Special to arrive on a blue plate, but it never did. Instead, it came on heavy, white stoneware. One dollar and ninety-nine cents got you a hefty slab of meatloaf with gravy, two sides, a garden salad, and a glass of sweetened iced tea. Even a twelve-year-old could afford that.

Bartley's Restaurant, situated on Madison Road between the Rescue Squad building and the A&P, was the ultimate in fine dining. Where else in town could you actually sit at a table and order from a real, plastic-coated menu? Where else could you get Roquefort dressing?

I don't remember much about Bartley's, but I do remember this: I remember Les and Charlotte, who ran the place. Les Bartley made a living for most of his life by providing Orange with good, solid fare. After Bartley's shut down he opened up The Airport Restaurant and later The Hilltop.

I also remember my buddy Gill and me trying to beat the heat on sweltering summer afternoons by spending an hour or so in the dark, air-conditioned sanctuary of Bartley's. We practiced acting sophisticated because we didn't often eat in "real" restaurants.

And I remember the Roquefort dressing. A creamy, white blob atop a plate of greens and sliced tomatoes. It probably came from a bottle, but I didn't know that then. I thought it was the best, and I ordered it every time.

To be fair, Bartley's wasn't the only true restaurant in Orange. There was also Devivi's. But Devivi's was out on Route 15, not really within walking distance for a town kid. Besides, it was Italian, and Italian meant exotic. Pizza and pasta, so common today, back then were delicacies, treats. We ate pizza once or twice a year; pasta—except for macaroni and cheese—almost never.

Devivi's was for special occasions, big evening dinners with large groups of friends. Bartley's was basic: a pork chop, beef stew, liver-and-onions kind of place.

Of course, if you wanted a light meal or a snack, you didn't need a restaurant at all; you just went to one of the drugstore lunch counters.

Grymes', Page's, or Rickett's—take your pick. I patronized them all.

Chicken salad on toast; hot dogs pressed flat on a foil-covered grilling iron; orangeade, squeezed from a huge steel juicer bolted to the counter; milk shakes and malts; burgers and fries; ham and cheese (American, of course, with or without pimento; who had heard of Swiss, Muenster or Provolone?) on white bread. Everything with chips and a pickle on the side. Sit on a stool at the counter, relax in a booth, or get your eats wrapped in wax paper to-go in a brown paper bag.

And though the food was good, the people were better.

Tommy Brown didn't work behind the lunch counter at Grymes, but he manned the main checkout. His bow-tie, smile, and gentlemanly conversation were reason enough to stop by for a Coke.

Bob and Peggy Gregg owned Page's and put their stamp of hospitality on everything in the place. (Just out of curiosity, can you tell me who "owns" a place like CVS or any of the mega-store pharmacies?)

And when you walked through the doors of Rickett's, either to grab a bite, to hang out after school, or just to pick up a box of Russell Stover candy for your mom's birthday, most likely you'd be met by Marshall Smith, looking like Teddy Roosevelt with his pipe clenched tightly between his teeth; or his wife Sue, bustling about, all energy, the store's real boss.

The death knell for drugstore lunch counters came with the arrival of the bypass. Suddenly, it was possible to go through Orange without going down Main Street. As businesses disappeared, so did the need for feeding people at lunch time.

Then came the shopping centers with their big chain pharmacies.

In Orange it was Drug Fair, a store that did employ good, friendly local people, but was owned by some impersonal entity in some vague place far away.

The store did have great stuff though. I bought my first Bob Dylan album at Drug Fair, as well as Fizzies, baseball cards, and countless comic books.

For a while it even had a few lunch booths in the back. But their heart wasn't really in it. Gill and I tried it a few times, but it was pretty disappointing. Sort of had the feel of a school cafeteria.

Such is progress.

It's Like, You Know

Not all English teachers are grammar Nazis. I don't correct my friends in public when they say "who" instead of "whom." I try to speak and write clearly myself, but I also try not to be obnoxious when others misspeak. Hearing "lay" when it should be "lie" hurts my ear, but I usually just let it go.

In the classroom I tend to correct my students gently, with humor. It's more effective; and besides, no one likes a grammar jerk.

One of the beauties of English is that it's flexible; it grows and adapts. The rules shift over time. What's incorrect today may become perfectly acceptable down the road. So, odd as it may sound coming from an English teacher, I tend not to get too bent out of shape over split infinitives, dangling modifiers, or prepositions at the ends of sentences.

But I'm about to draw the line. The word "like" is driving me stark, raving mad. Most of my students cannot speak for thirty seconds without larding their speech with half a dozen "likes." These are kids who will soon be going off to good colleges. They're intelligent; they'll score high on the SAT; and they are nice, pleasant people. In normal, face-to-face conversation, however, they are grotesquely inarticulate.

A typical classroom scenario goes something like this:

Mr. Amos: Tell me, what do you think Yeats means when he says "the best lack all conviction"?

Typical Student: I think he's like saying like, the best people are like, not very like full of like, you know, conviction."

I'm not exaggerating.

And outside of class, in the hallways, it's even worse. Not a day goes by that I don't overhear some version of the following:

"I was like, 'No way.' And then he was like, 'What?' And so I was like, 'Whatever.'"

It's become habitual. Most of them don't even realize what they're saying. Only when I call it to their attention do they consider how ridiculous they sound. Even then, many are unable to stop themselves. It embarrasses them that they can't control their addiction, but not so much that they're willing to do anything about it.

One of my strengths as a teacher is that I know how to conduct a lively discussion. I'm pretty good at getting kids to talk about things that matter. However, more and more, my discussions with kids about literature and life are so infected by the "like" virus that no one really knows what anyone else is saying.

So I'm taking a stand. I'm starting a crusade. From this moment on, my classroom will be one hundred percent "like-free." My students will learn to slow down, think about what they want to say, and then say it. Or else.

If I have to, I'll hit them in the one area I know they really care about: their grades. I'm disgusted, I'm angry, and I'm not putting up with it anymore. I may not accomplish anything else for the next year or so; but I'm going to attack this problem, even if it's only in my little corner of the world.

Listen: These are not just the ravings of an old curmudgeon with a bee in his bonnet about "kids these days."

I really worry that my students' attachment to the word "like" may cripple them permanently. I don't think this is just a passing fad. I can picture them ten or fifteen years down the road, trying to tell their children a story and not being able to muster more than, "Once upon a time, there were like, these three like, little pig-things . . ."

I've become a fan in recent years of George Orwell. Most people know him as the author of *Animal Farm* and *1984*, but I've grown especially fond of his essays. No one writes with such precision or such economy of language. In Orwell every word matters.

In his essay "Politics and the English Language" Orwell contends that fuzzy speech is a reflection of fuzzy thinking. Modern English, he says, "is full of bad habits which spread by imitation . . .If one gets rid of these habits, one can think more clearly."

He closes the essay by advocating all-out war on lazy, imprecise language. It's possible, he argues, to effect change through ridicule. "One can, if one jeers loudly enough, send some worn-out and useless phrase, some lump of verbal refuse, into the dustbin where it belongs."

Look out, "like." Here I come.

THE LOST ART

I wrote the assignment on the board, white chalk on black slate. When the kid in the back row asked me to read it aloud, I was worried that he might need glasses. So I asked him. His answer floored me: "I can see fine; I just can't read cursive."

During my twenty-seven years as an English teacher I've watched cursive handwriting gradually disappear among high-school students. The majority prefer to type on the word-processor; but if forced to write by hand, they almost always choose print over cursive. Still, I wasn't prepared for a student to admit so casually that he couldn't read a simple set of instructions. I didn't realize it had gotten quite so bad.

As a high-school teacher I've not been in a position to do much more than bewail the trend. My students were exposed to cursive a long time ago in grade school, but they were never required to use it. The habit was never ingrained in them. And so they have opted for "easier" print over the vastly more efficient—and more beautiful—cursive.

I suppose if I wanted to drop everything else, I could spend all my time teaching the dying art of handwriting. I could quit teaching literature, composition, grammar and vocabulary. I could forego prepping students for the SAT. It would take all of my time, but I could "go old-school" on my students, forcing them to learn what they should have learned long ago. But what would be the point? Why teach a skill that's rapidly becoming obsolete?

I hate to say it, but good handwriting is no longer necessary. It's a luxury, a frill. You really can get by today without having to write much by hand. In fact, I'm hard-pressed to think of a job which still requires good penmanship. Even the term "penmanship" has an old-fashioned ring to it.

There was a time when my best students had the best handwriting. But that's no longer the case. Some of my sharpest kids can produce no better than a sort of scribbled henscratch on the page. Some have even been diagnosed with "disgraphia," an official learning disability that, as far as I can tell, means they can't write neatly.

Certainly, the death of handwriting has coincided with the rise of the computer. After all, typed, electronic communication accounts for nearly all of the writing that most people do. We don't need to write, and so we don't. And though I spend a good bit of time railing against technology, when it comes to its effect on writing, I'm ambivalent. I actually love the computer as a writer's tool.

I recall my college days when I wrote everything by hand and typed afterwards. I'd sit at my desk with a legal pad, pen, and a pair of scissors, trying to compose an essay on Tennyson's "In Memoriam" or Chaucer's *Canterbury Tales*. I'd write a while, revise a while, then ball up the page, toss it aside, and start over again. After a few paragraphs I'd start rearranging, literally cutting and pasting with scissors and tape. Writing back then was a tedious and frustrating affair.

The computer makes the process so much easier. Good writers revise, revise, and then revise again. For me, the joy of writing is in the revising. I love cutting this and adding that; I love fiddling with phrases until they're just right. The computer allows me to revise more frequently and more comprehensively, so I stand a better chance of getting an idea across clearly than I do with pen and paper. I'm a better writer because of, not in spite of, the computer.

Still, I mourn for what's been lost.

I think of monks in the Middle Ages and their gorgeous illuminated manuscripts.

. . . of Anthony Trollope, the great nineteenth century novelist, who wrote 3,000 words a day by hand.

. . . of John Hancock's signature on the Declaration.

. . . of the cool, backwards slant of left-handers.

. . . of the Briffaux twins, boys from Belgium I taught years ago, who attributed their graceful script to beatings delivered by schoolmasters who insisted on neatness.

. . . of handwritten notes from friends, real ink on real paper.

. . . and of my own signature, which intentionally runs my middle initial "B" into the "A" of my last name.

Maybe I'll start a new organization: the SPCCA. The Society for the Preservation of Cursive in the Computer Age. Only one membership requirement: concern for how to revive a dying art.

GEORGE

I spoke with George Darnell the other night.
I hadn't seen him in years. In fact, he died back in
'97, which obviously made all normal conversation
impossible.

But then he showed up again. In my dream. And
we talked.

Most dreams are forgettable. They're gone before
your feet hit the floor in the morning. Bits and pieces
may return while you're drinking your coffee or but-
tering your toast, but by noon the details are lost for
good.

Real dreams—the ones that matter—never fade.
They are moments of sheer grace, flashing out of nowhere and shining with such rare beauty that the mind
feels their imprint forever.

You're blessed with only a few such dreams in a
lifetime. My dream of George the other night was of
this sort.

I hadn't been thinking of him, hadn't spoken of
him to anyone, couldn't even tell you the last time he'd

crossed my mind. Yet there he was—alive and real, as impish and full of nonsense as ever. A little Hobbit of a man, with toothbrush eyebrows, a graceful ski-slope nose, and eyes that twinkled with serious mischief.

It was so good to chat. I didn't realize how much I'd missed the old buster.

I first met George when I was a teenager, working on a truck-farm behind Miss Caine's old place. He had long since retired from Safeway. Every day, as I pulled weeds, he puttered around in his own little patch between the corn and potato fields. Only about five and half feet tall, he looked a bit like a garden gnome come to life as he hoed, watered, planted, and tilled in the hot sun.

He did, in fact, have a gnomish sense of humor. I once asked him why he carried a second hoe to the garden every day. His answer was classic.

"Because, boy. I work so fast that one might overheat. I use the second while the first one's cooling off." Grin. Wink. Eye-sparkle.

The man was full of such stuff.

"Hey, George. How'd you get those tomatoes to grow so big?"

"The secret's in the bootsun-dootsun, boy. Horse bootsun-dootsun is good, but rabbit bootsun-dootsun is best."

Thirty-five years later, as I mix up Miracle-Gro for the marigolds, I think, "Let's see what an extra shot of bootsun-dootsun will do."

He carried his green thumb back from the garden to his little white stucco house in town. With a grape arbor in the backyard and a front yard full of poppies and larkspur, roses climbing up trellises and potted geraniums all around, 127 Belleview was clearly the playground of a master garden putterer.

When he wasn't gardening, he was tooling around town in a beaten up old white Chevrolet, running errands for his wife Myrie—errands that usually involved looking for sales at the dollar store or comparison shopping between the Safeway and A&P.

George once offered me a ride home in that rattletrap. I know I'm prone to exaggeration, but this is the God's honest truth: the inside of his car was so full of newspapers and sales fliers that my head hit the ceiling. It was like sitting on half a dozen phone books.

Toward the end of his life, George was the victim of a great tragedy. One night a thief broke into the Virginia Metals plant where he was working as a night watchman and beat him up pretty badly. I'm not sure that he ever fully recovered, physically or emotionally. The last time I chatted with him, on the steps of the post office, he seemed a bit distant. He still carried on a little of the old nonsense, but clearly some of the spark was gone.

That's why it was so wonderful to see him the other night.

A dream scene: *A potluck supper at the Methodist Church. The fellowship hall is jammed with people, standing shoulder-to-shoulder around tables loaded with ham biscuits, baked beans and Jell-O salads. George sits in a chair, Myrie by his side. He calls me over. I bend down and he grabs my face with both hands.*

His voice is strong, his smile broad, his eyes full

of light. "Boy," he says. "What are you doing here?"

"Just came to see you, George."

A peal of mischievous laughter. A wink. Lots of eye-sparkle.

"Glad you did, boy."

So am I, George. So am I.

CUSSIN' THE COMICS

I'm no fan of the "dark" comics. Every now and then, I'll turn to the funny pages and check out "Blondie" or "Beetle Bailey" or some such nonsense. But I never bother with the dark, serious ones, the ones printed with lots of black ink, like "Rex Morgan" and "Judge Parker" and "Mary Worth."

That's not to say I don't know about the dark ones. Between my wife and my father, two real comic-crazies, I manage to keep up. I get it all secondhand by overhearing their weekly phone calls.

I'm puzzled sometimes at how two extremely intelligent people can take this stuff seriously. My wife graduated Phi Beta Kappa with a degree in Slavic languages. My father is one of the most well-read people I know. And yet to hear them on the phone, talking breathlessly about the latest happenings in "Mark Trail," you'd think they were two teenagers discussing hot gossip.

At least once a week they call each other to yap about the villain stalking Mary Worth or whether Mark Trail is going to catch the poacher with the really bad sideburns.

This'll tell you something: These two actually missed "Apartment 3-G" when it disappeared from the *Washington Post* a few years ago. And they can tell you everything you ever wanted to know about Prince Valiant, Dick Tracy, or Winnie Winkle. Go figure.

When the *Post* temporarily dropped "Mark Trail" awhile back, they both flew into a righteous rage. High, high dudgeon ensued. How dare they!

My dad has been a comics fanatic for as long as I can remember. His love-hate relationship with "Brenda Starr, Star Reporter" tended to dominate our breakfast table conversation when I was growing up, especially on Sunday mornings when Brenda was at her most syrupy. This was the strip he loved to hate. I can still hear him, toast in one hand and coffee in the other, ranting about "the frustrated old biddy" who drew the redheaded reporter with the beauty mark on her cheek. He hated the strip's sappiness and melodrama. But he kept on reading.

I thought he'd finally give it up when Brenda married Basil St. John, the mysterious guy with the eye-patch. (They named their first child Starr Twinkle). But he stuck it out. He thought it utter tripe, but he read on faithfully.

My wife has been a comics fan since childhood. I'm not sure when she got hooked on the "dark" ones, but hooked she is.

We get the *Post* delivered daily, and I read the sports, the op-eds, and even the Metro section on occasion. But the real reason we subscribe is that my wife needs the comics page. It's her pressure valve.

She works two jobs, hauls kids from here to there, manages the family finances (such as they are), quilts and knits in every spare minute, and generally keeps our family on an even keel. She's a woman with a busy life.

A voracious reader, she watches very little television, preferring instead to get her entertainment from books and comic strips.

For her, the dark comics are a sort of soap-opera substitute. She hasn't got time to lounge around eating bonbons and watching *As the World Turns* everyday. So, it's ten minutes in the morning over breakfast with Mark and Mary and Sam Driver.

I can't really account for the fact that I've never caught the comics-bug myself. As a kid I spent hours reading *Richie Rich, Archie*, and *Superman*. I love old pulp fiction and even the new, cutting edge graphic novels. Though I try to teach quality literature, I'm a big fan of cheesy, plot-driven stories as well. You'd think I'd be a prime candidate for following the funny papers.

Maybe it's just that, as an adult, I've had no reason to read them. I can get the scoop just by listening in from the fringes.

You hope when you get married that your parents will love and accept the person you've chosen to spend your life with. You don't really know, but you hope.

What you could never predict is that a buzz-cut, tough-guy cop and a brainy girl with a passion for needlework will have a mutual love for "Mary Worth," "Mark Trail," and "Spiderman." I don't pretend to understand. I just listen in, smile, and shake my head.

It must be a father-daughter sort of thing.

JINKS

For Mark and Phil, because you knew him best.

If you chew tobacco, you need a spit cup. Of course, if you're like my grandfather, it'll mostly be for show. Granddaddy usually spat in the general direction of the Maxwell House can he kept beside his chair. If he hit it, fine. If not, that was okay too.

He was a man with clear preferences in his choice of tobacco. He chewed plugs of Thick Apple only. He wanted nothing to do with the light, leafy stuff in pouches. I'm not sure I ever saw him without a brick of Thick Apple in his pocket.

This—and his preference for King Edward cigars—made him easy to shop for. A case of Thick Apple or a five-pack of cheap stogies became standard Christmas and birthday presents. (Someone once made the mistake of giving him a box of "real" cigars. He merely traded them away for King Edwards, which my father swears are made of clippings swept from the factory floor.)

In my family nicknames abound. Aunt Myrtle was

"Charlie." Elizabeth was "Jack." Stella was "Bootie." Luther was "Kneed." My great-grandparents were "Miss Willie" and "Beely." Somehow William Ellis Amos became "Jinks." I'd love to hear the story behind the name, but no one seems to know. Just another one of those things now lost forever.

This I do know. My grandfather was a worker. I wasn't around during his early years in Rapidan; but even when he was well past his prime, his chest and hands let you know that this was a man who understood physical labor.

I remember him mostly in his "retirement." Clad in bow tie and bald head shining, he stood for years behind the counter in Sam Duggins' Western Auto. Later he moved to Faulconer's Hardware. Well into his seventies he worked as janitor for the Orange Baptist Church, mopping floors, setting up chairs for meetings, and cleaning bathrooms.

Unlike many retirees, he never took a job simply to keep himself busy. Southern Railroad had rewarded his many years of service with a pitifully small monthly check, so he needed to keep working to get by. If it bothered him, I never knew.

Actions really do speak louder than words. I never received any grandfatherly lectures about the importance of work. Never any speeches about bringing dignity to every job. He never said, "Boy, you must always work hard, whatever the task." There was no need to preach that sermon because he lived it so clearly.

It used to bother me that my grandfather never owned his own home. That so much work could result in so little material gain still seems unfair to me. When he died, he left behind a few scraps of worn out furniture in a rented apartment, a few pots and pans, some clothes, and not much else. However, my grandfather's life is truly a testament to the fact that things don't really matter much.

Just ask my brother or my nephew, both of whom spent a good portion of their teenage years hanging out at my granddad's place after Grandmama died. Ask them if a kid really cares who owns the house? Ask them whether an old man needs a lot of money to keep a grandson entertained. They'll answer like this:

As long as you can stay up late watching professional wrestling (and cuss the referee for failing to see Rip Hawk conceal a foreign object in his trunks), as long as you can ride to the A&P in a rundown gold Impala with a sun-blistered leather roof, as long as you can drink strong coffee and read the paper over a breakfast of bacon and fried eggs (good fried eggs require a cast-iron skillet and at least an inch of bacon grease), as long as you can coo over the tabby cat that has the run of the place, as long as you can spit tobacco juice at a tin can and not worry about whether you hit it, as long as you can do all this with your granddad, does anything else really matter?

Granddaddy's life was undeniably hard, but it didn't make him hard. There was not a jot of bitterness in him. No resentment. No meanness. No sense that the world owed him more. A simple man with simple tastes, all he ever needed was a job to do, a grandkid to spend time with, and a plug of Thick Apple.

GONE BUT NOT FORGOTTEN

Can you miss someone you never even knew? Sure, you can. I never really knew John Duffey; but when he died, the loss I felt was profound and real. I still miss him, though he's been gone now for years.

Duffey was bluegrass royalty. A mandolin player extraordinaire, he teamed up with Charlie Waller in the late '50s to form The Country Gentlemen. The two of them, along with bassist Tom Gray and banjo picker Eddie Adcock, revolutionized traditional mountain music with their bluegrass renderings of contemporary country, folk, and pop songs.

Later, after leaving Waller's band, Duffey founded The Seldom Scene, an even more progressive bluegrass group that specialized in what he laughingly called "Acid Grass." Every concert included not only beautiful gospel harmonies and updated versions of Ralph Stanley classics, but also hard-driving bluegrass takes on rock 'n' roll: J. J. Cale's "After Midnight," Clapton's "Lay Down Sally," and the like. Their show even featured a Hendrix-like dobro solo from Mike Auldridge, complete with feedback effects. Here were middle-aged men playing *my* music on *their* instruments. It was sort of like The Grand Old Opry and Woodstock all rolled into one.

I first heard John Duffey in the early 1980s. Before my kids were born, my wife and I used to make regular Thursday night visits to Alexandria to hear The Seldom Scene play live at The Birchmere, an intimate little listening club where, if you arrived early, you could sit close enough to prop your feet on the stage.

The band consisted of five terrific musicians, but the star was clearly the big guy with the mandolin. At six-feet three-inches tall, he seemed far too large to pick so tiny an instrument with such speed and precision.

Moreover, he was a really odd duck. Decked out in his trademark Hawaiian bowling shirt, his silver hair cut in a high flattop, sporting sharp Mafioso sideburns, he simply dominated the stage. Ever the ham, he delighted in turning up his collar Elvis-style, making bawdy comments, and telling bad jokes. (A favorite was to ask the audience for applause after an extended spell of tuning his instrument, claiming that he'd just played an old Chinese folk song called "Tu-Ning.") He exuded charisma and he compelled attention. The others were good, but your eyes just naturally gravitated toward Duffey.

His goofy shtick didn't really matter though. What mattered was his voice.

John Duffey's voice was a razor. It could cut you;

it sliced into you. When he wanted, he could draw blood. And like a razor, his voice cut smoothly and deeply without your even knowing it. The wound didn't hurt right away, but afterwards you definitely felt the ache.

Bill Monroe may have invented the "high lonesome sound," but John Duffey perfected it. He sang what I've heard described as "whiskey tenor," simultaneously raw and polished, pure and ragged, sharp and silky. His unearthly high notes on the folk tune "500 Miles" raised the hair on the back of your neck and gave you gooseflesh. His voice defined "lonely."

You can still hear him, of course. Country Gentlemen records are easy to find, and The Seldom Scene put out lots of music that's well worth listening to. Old *Train, Baptizing,* and *Live at the Cellar Door* should be part of every music lover's collection. Still, recorded music can't really match the live experience.

It's Thursday night. We're sitting at a small table just at the edge of the stage. The waitress brings our order of fried shrimp and onion rings in red-checkered baskets. As I reach for money to pay her, the yellow footlights fade to blue. A white spot pierces the smoke, illuminating a tall man in a bowling shirt. He steps to the microphone. For a moment time freezes. A hush descends. The waitress kneels quietly beside our table, waiting till the song's over to complete the transaction out of respect for the musicians. The band begins: first dobro, then guitar, mandolin, banjo and bass. A high, haunting voice sings a slit in the darkness: "Wait a minute. Did I hear you say you're going far away again? Try to change it. I can't face the lonely nights . . ." The song hurts my heart.

It's been nine years since John Duffey died, too young, at age sixty-two. When I read the news in the paper, I just sat there, stunned. I didn't really know him. But, my goodness, I miss him.

HOOP DREAMS

Picture JR, a tall lanky, sensitive kid who loves basketball and has some talent.

Now picture a typical high-school practice session,
sneakers squeaking on the gym floor as boys scrim-
mage and the coach looks on. At one point, the coach
blows his whistle and stops the action. He's not happy.

"Listen," he sneers at JR. "If you can't stick with
him, just hook your finger in his jock strap and hang
on for the ride."

Never mind that he's assigned the boy to guard a
kid half his size and twice as quick. Never mind that
he has him playing a position he hasn't played all season. Never mind that he hasn't taught him even the
rudiments of how to play defense. All that matters is
that JR just let a guy go by him for a lay-up . . . twice.

He's a screamer, this coach. One of those tough
guys who motivate by fear. An in-your-face, chew-
your-butt, cuss-you-out drill sergeant. Do what I say,
do it now, and don't ask questions.

JR has learned to expect screaming, so he worries this time when his coach sneers snidely instead of yells. Apparently, the boy's game is so pathetic that he doesn't deserve even a good chewing out, just a wicked dose of cutting, dismissive sarcasm. The kid senses right then, down in his gut, that his season is over. Sure enough, he rides the bench for the next dozen games.

If you want proof that kids are impressionable, and that coaches and teachers must watch what they say, incidents like this should suffice. They happen every day. And their effect lingers, for decades, even with people who don't normally hold grudges.

Coaches are essentially teachers. The best are innovative, creative, and infinitely patient. They inspire loyalty. And they're demanding, forever challenging their players to do and be their best.

The worst are dull, unimaginative, capricious, and often—intentionally or unintentionally—cruel. Add a touch of ego and you've got the potential for something really nasty.

The truly bad ones, the screamers, justify their behavior by insisting that they're simply teaching kids toughness, to be winners at life. They forget that words can just as easily kill the spirit as lift it.

Conventional wisdom says that playing a sport "builds character." Hogwash. Playing a sport *reveals* character. And that's an entirely different matter.

On the football field, the baseball diamond, or the basketball court, you find out what people are really made of. It doesn't take long to discover who's selfish and who's lazy; who's resilient and who's loyal; who's humble and who's arrogant. If you want to find out who cheats and who doesn't, just spend a few hours on a golf course.

Fact: Games show how people act under pressure, but games cannot make people into something they're not.

Certainly, a good coach can have a tremendously positive influence on a kid's life. And a bad coach can do incredible damage. Neither, however, can change a person's essential character. It just can't happen.

I was required early in my career as an independent school teacher to coach basketball, baseball, and soccer. I wasn't any good at it. In fact, I was awful and got out as soon as I could. I just didn't have the temperament.

As a player, I hated to lose—and still do. Oddly, as a coach it didn't seem to bother me that much.

As a player, I loved the feeling of "being in the zone;" but as a coach, everything felt out of sync. Always. Somehow I couldn't make myself care as much as I should have.

To be honest, I sometimes wonder if kids wouldn't be better off without coaches. I go through phases where I think maybe we ought to ban all adults from what should be kids' games.

Picture JR, a tall lanky, sensitive kid who loves basketball and has some talent.

Now picture a typical outdoor playground with kids racing up and down the blacktop, shots swishing through chain-metal nets or clanging off rusty steel backboards. The game's an intense, run-and-gun affair. Players on both teams shout good-natured trash at their opponents.

No coaches pace the sidelines, ordering instructions or micromanaging the action. No one gets pulled
for missing an assignment. No silly substitutions. No
ridiculous time-outs because there is no clock. No
screaming matches with referees because there're none
of them either.

It's just a game. Kids playing. Absolutely pure.
Absolutely simple. The way it ought to be.

GRANDDADDY BO

Something surely must have hurt him.

He had farmer's hands that knew how to work the dirt. With his handsome cragged face, huge pendulous ears, and dignified shock of downy white hair, he always reminded me a little of poet Robert Frost. At six feet tall and raw-boned, he certainly looked strong enough to withstand almost anything. But appearances deceive. Of all my grandparents, Granddaddy Bo was by far the most fragile.

I use vague generalities here because I don't actually know the truth. I'm not really sure I want to know, anyway. Only this matters: Life sometimes hits hard, and the fragile break easily. Somewhere along the line, Granddaddy was almost broken. At the very least, his spirit was pretty badly bruised.

The result was a silent enigma of a man, so withdrawn and wary of the world that he preferred to live life from a rocking chair in his own living room.

He and Grandmama Mary were my "country" grandparents. They owned a sort of mini-farm just a little way down the Brampton Road. This is where you went if you wanted to pick the snakeberries that grew in the ditch next to the driveway, or fly a kite in the field that fronted Route 15, collect hickory nuts or hunt fool's gold, race cousins to "the fir tree" and back, or play hide-and-seek in the cornfields.

Situated on little more than an acre, their place had all the elements of a full-fledged farm: a meathouse, dark and musty, smelling of sugar-cured hams and smoky slabs of peppered bacon; a chicken coop, used mostly for raising those squawking, speckled guinea hens; and a board-fence pigpen, the mud and muck inside littered with corncobs, acorns, and slop from Grandmama's kitchen.

Mary Colvin understood work. She earned her living first at the Woodberry Forest laundry and later as a saleswoman in the basement of Leggett's Department Store.

I'm sure it was her earnings and her determination that allowed my grandparents to buy property and build a home in the first place. In addition to such jobs outside the house, Grandmama also kept everything running smoothly back home: sewing, cooking, cleaning, gardening, mowing, raking, burning trash, and taking care of the animals.

Granddaddy Bo, on the other hand, didn't work at all. He sat. Or he slept. As a young man he had worked on farms, maybe even managed a few. And when I was a youngster, I vaguely remember him working for a while at a local building supply. But the grandfather I knew mostly sat around the house, rocking in the living room chair or napping in a back bedroom.

He didn't read newspapers, books or magazines. He almost never watched television. He didn't listen to music or play an instrument. He didn't attend church. He didn't own a dog or follow sports. I'm pretty sure he didn't have a driver's license. And he rarely initiated a conversation.

He wasn't lazy. And he wasn't really sick, at least not in the common sense of that word. In an era that didn't make such diagnoses, he probably suffered from depression. I don't really know; but in retrospect, it seems likely.

Children observe closely, but they don't often judge. Granddaddy Bo's behavior didn't strike me as odd until much later, when I looked back through adult eyes. As a boy, I just loved him, as every boy loves his grandfather.

I loved that he nicknamed me "Baptist." I loved that he bought the "staples" whenever he went grocery shopping (He let grandmama buy the "frills," while his job was to stock up on flour, sugar, butter, eggs, and milk). I loved that he was a country-ham critic, always the best judge of how well the holiday meat had been cooked. I loved that he paid me a quarter to scratch his head. I loved that he called my grandmother "Sister," and that he intentionally took out his hearing aid whenever company dropped by. I loved that he sharpened his garden hoe on a huge pedal-powered grindstone. I loved that he actually preferred raisins with seeds, that he called potatoes "taters," and that he enjoyed big midday meals. I loved that he wore bib overalls and ate onions straight out of the garden. I loved that he laughed at my jokes.

How to make sense of such a life? I can't. I simply rejoice that the hurt which bent him so severely didn't entirely break him.

Taking Care

Parents were terrified. The abduction of a young woman from her car while traveling a local highway had the whole town on edge. Likewise, the mysterious disappearance of two young girls in a neighboring county had brought a kind of unease I'd never known. Small towns are supposed to be immune from this kind of terror, but now everyone wanted to keep the kids close by.

At the time, my own children were fairly small. Their favorite gathering place was a clubhouse they'd built in a lot just off Main Street. I'd given them some old lumber, a hammer and nails, and a leftover scrap of carpet. Along with the neighbor's kids, they'd scrounged up other materials and constructed a sort of ramshackle hovel. To them, however, it was "The Fort"—a glorious place with its own rules, completely apart from the intruding presence of adults. They routinely spent entire summer days at "The Fort."

They thought they were alone, but they weren't. Not really. Every half-hour or so, I'd go out and check on them, often standing just far enough away to hear them without their suspecting anyone was nearby. I hated doing it, but I couldn't help myself. Kids were disappearing, and I had to know that mine were safe.

I think my children, when they look back, will describe their childhood years as carefree, maybe even idyllic. For the most part, they've been allowed to grow up in a safe neighborhood, their days filled with fun and friends. And yet, as a parent, I have a nagging sense that I've been required by the realities of modern life to keep them a little too sheltered.

Certainly I've prohibited them from doing things that my own parents never thought twice about.

As a fourteen-year-old, I regularly rode my bicycle from Orange to Madison Mills so that I could float down the river in an inner tube. To my knowledge, bike helmets hadn't been invented. (Besides, any self-respecting boy wouldn't have been caught dead in such a geeky looking thing.) Cars on Route 15 whizzed by at top speeds, and on the long downhill slopes I pedaled my hardest, trying to keep up with them.

Looking back, it was an incredibly dangerous thing; and had I wiped out even once along the way, chances are I wouldn't be writing this today. But I never remember my parents forbidding me to go. In fact, I never remember even asking my parents' permission to go. A kid wants to ride his bike to the river? No big deal. That's what kids do.

Once, my mother let me catch a Trailways bus to Charlottesville with a friend to see the latest martial arts movie. I think I was in the seventh grade. After the matinee, we spent the rest of the afternoon wandering around downtown, riding the bank elevator and eating ice cream. We caught the bus back home at the edge of dark.

If my own kids ever asked to do such a thing, I'd look at them as though they had three heads. They'd get the lecture: Times are just too dangerous. It would be irresponsible of me as a parent to let you go. Who knows what might happen alone on a bus?

And yet, something tells me that such an attitude shrinks the imaginative possibilities of childhood. I can't get past the feeling that, in the name of keeping my children safe, I've kept them from fully being kids.

Even when I have allowed them their freedom, I've found myself saying over and over, "Be careful." Sure, you can walk to the store. Just be careful. You can go over to so-and-so's. Just be careful. You can do this, that, or the other. Just be careful. The injunction to "take care" has been a huge part of my parenting vocabulary.

In an ideal world, kids wouldn't have to "take care." They'd be completely carefree: floating down the river in an inner tube, no lifejacket; flying down the highway, helmet-less, on a bike; flopping in the back of a station wagon without the seat belts; hanging upside down from the monkey bars with only the hard blacktop below; lighting bottle rockets without adult supervision; skating down the sidewalk without knee or elbow pads; just being kids.

I know it's my job to keep them safe; but for their own sake, I wish I didn't have to care so much.

The Honey Wagon, etc.

It took me a few minutes to realize what the guy was doing.

While driving to the post office the other day, I spied this fellow standing precariously atop a stepladder on the side of the road, a hat pulled over his eyes to shield him from the sun. He seemed about to make a public proclamation of some sort to a crowd that wasn't there. Then I saw the paintbrush in his hand and realized he was painting signposts. Memories came flooding back.

In the summer of 1974 my buddy Randy and I signed on to work with the maintenance crew for the Town of Orange. Each year, when school ended, the Department of Public Works hired a couple of teenagers as extra hands. I've always known that education doesn't only happen in the schoolhouse, but that summer proved it to me emphatically. I gained more practical knowledge working for the town than I ever did in a classroom.

Much of our time was spent hacking weeds with a sickle, sweeping sidewalks, and hosing debris from the picnic shelter at Porterfield. But our most glamorous job by far was painting the NO-PARKING curbs along Main Street.

For most of a week, in blistering July sun, we sat cross-legged in the gutter, a bucket of fluorescent yellow paint in one hand, a paintbrush in the other, waving at passing traffic and basking in the attention of local passersby. Just a glimpse of the man on the stepladder the other day sent me time-traveling. Thirty-plus years melted in the blink of an eye.

The jobs we performed were myriad and included riding the back of the trash truck, digging ditches for water lines, constructing storm drains, and pouring concrete for new curb and gutter. Hot, dirty work it was; but when we finished, we'd accomplished something. A street was noticeably cleaner. A neighborhood had been improved. Being young and inexperienced, I didn't realize that few jobs yield such tangible results.

Among other things, working for the town taught me to drive. I had my license, of course, and had tooled around town for months in my sister's old blue Mustang. But that summer I regularly got assigned to the town's green one-ton dump truck. I didn't have a clue about how to operate such a vehicle, but when the superintendent put me on "brush duty," I learned on the fly.

Every Wednesday I'd hop behind the wheel of the old weather-beaten ton-truck, Randy riding shotgun, and head through town, collecting curbside brush to haul to the landfill. On rainy days we'd kill time at the dump by intentionally sinking our back wheels in the mud so that the bulldozer operator could rescue us with his chain. (As they say, "Your tax dollars at work.")

We didn't quite know what to expect, however, when we got assigned to spend a week at the sewer plant.

Let's see if I can describe this accurately: Our job was to pitchfork dried, processed sewage from large beds of sand into the "honey wagon," where it would be hauled off to . . . I'm not sure where.

It wasn't exactly fun, but we survived and even managed to keep our sense of humor about it. After a long morning of shoveling sludge we were, you might say, a bit fragrant. We'd head back to town for lunch, usually stopping at the Safeway deli for Polish sausage and fried potato wedges. Instead of hiding our aroma, we gloried in it, laughing at the upturned noses of little old ladies in line behind us.

All of this earned us $2.50 an hour. A hundred bucks for a forty-hour week, minus twelve dollars in taxes. To a sixteen-year-old in 1974, an eighty-eight dollar paycheck qualified as riches. What I didn't realize, of course, was that the full-time employees, guys who worked at the shop year round, were being paid only a little more. How they supported families on such a pittance I'll never know.

I'm sure my students think I'm crazy; but if I could, I'd require them all to work a job like this. They could use a few lessons in the importance of physical labor. They could benefit from a job that teaches them the value of money and the necessity of following directions, the importance of being on time and of doing even an unpleasant task well.

Loading the "honey wagon" for a few days would be just the ticket.

AM I MY BROTHER'S KEEPER?

Whoever designed the place knew what they were doing. Built to resemble a 1930's railway station, the Holocaust Memorial Museum in Washington, D.C., forces you, from the moment you enter the building, to confront what happened.

Most museums seem somewhat haphazard in their layout, and so encourage a haphazard approach to viewing. My tendency upon entering a museum is to wander aimlessly from exhibit to exhibit, reading bits of informational blurbs, but mostly just skimming and moving on.

In truth, I've never been a big fan of museums. I love art galleries, but I'm really not all that impressed by dark rooms filled with dinosaur bones, mummies, and huge blue diamonds. They're lifeless places, with history preserved behind sealed glass panes.

But the Holocaust Museum is different.

The museum is organized by decade, from the top down: the third floor covers the 1930s and the rise of Hitler and anti-Semitism in Germany. The second floor documents the war years and the atrocities committed by the Nazis against Jews in Europe. The ground floor is dominated by The Hall of Remembrance, a large, open, circular space with benches where visitors can rest, think, pray, or simply be. Such a plan discourages the kind of aimless wandering I'm prone to.

Upon arrival, you receive an identity card with biographical information about a particular Holocaust victim. Mine was of a teen-aged boy, David, gassed at Dachau. In this way the museum forces you to view tragic history in the most personal terms.

You then travel via elevator to the third floor and begin to work your way down. Once inside, you can't really escape. Everything about the museum—from the heartbreaking photographs of Jewish victims to the piles of shoes taken at concentration camps to the videotaped interviews with survivors—forces you to confront the question: How can human beings do such evil?

It's an emotionally draining, spiritually exhausting experience. Clearly, this is not a place to visit casually.

I first toured the museum in the late '90s as part of a professional development seminar. A curator lectured our group about how "this museum is different" and how it requires teachers to prepare their students before bringing them on field trips.

She told of students running wild through the museum, making-out in the boxcar exhibit, laughing and shouting inappropriately during their tours. Her point was that the Holocaust Museum is not the Air and Space Museum, not the Museum of Natural History, and certainly not the zoo.

Teachers, she insisted, need to think about why they are bringing students to such a place. (I would extend her argument to cover all field trips. Teachers too often take kids places without offering any context for the trip, without helping them connect what they're seeing to what they've been doing in class.)

The Holocaust Museum itself recognizes that it may not be an appropriate place for children. Because the Nazis documented so much of their horrific work on camera, the museum contains a number of video exhibits. Wisely, the curators have chosen to position video monitors on the floor, facing up, surrounded by a waist-high wall. This way, small children may see the exhibit only if their parents choose to lift them above the wall.

It's a touchy issue, how to tell children about such evil.

I still remember my own daughter, at the age of nine, crying one night after having inadvertently seen a short clip about concentration camps on the History Channel. What exactly does a father say in a situation where telling the truth seems as bad as lying? Do you tell her that the pile of bodies she saw isn't real? That the Holocaust happened a long time ago? That she's safe and nothing like that will ever happen to her? How do you restore a kid's innocence once she's seen the pictures?

I'm sitting on a bench in The Hall of Remembrance, alone, numb. The last three hours have overwhelmed. The pictures have been too much. One stays with me: a young girl, naked, ribs and shoulders protruding, hollowed-eyed. *She's about my daughter's age.*

I look up.

WHAT HAVE YOU DONE? YOUR BROTHER'S BLOOD CRIES OUT TO ME FROM THE GROUND, *reads the inscription on the wall. God to Cain after the murder of Abel.*

Cain's response, snide and sneering, is not written on the wall, but its presence hangs in the room nevertheless, demanding an answer.

"Am I my brother's keeper?"

Gods of the Copybook Headings

Here's a test. It's not hard: five questions, all with the same answer.

1. How can a ten-year-old child know the lyrics to dozens of rap songs but not know a single story from either the Old or New Testaments?
2. How can a middle-class adult spend more than twenty hours a week watching television but "not have time" for community service?
3. Why are most American children more skilled at playing video games than they are at using a shovel?
4. How did we get to the point where only one in three American households has a resident, married father?
5. Why do more people vote for American Idol than for president of the United States?

The answer to these (and a thousand others like them) is simple: our values are screwy, our priorities outrageously out of whack. We've put the emphasis on all the wrong things, and the result has been tragic.

Family, faith, civic responsibility, work ethic? Who teaches this stuff anymore? Nobody, as far as I can tell. We've fallen down on the job.

Can we fix what's broken? I'm not sure, but I think a return to the days of the copybook might be in order. In the nineteenth century, students were required to keep a sort of notebook or primer, in which they copied, over and over, a series of basic moral precepts.

"Afflictions are often blessings in disguise."

"Eschew evil; cling to what is good."

"By its fruit a tree is known."

"The wages of sin is death."

The idea was to help students improve their penmanship and at the same time to instill some basic moral truths about life and living.

How quaint: that a teacher would be concerned with a child's moral education. Wonder when that idea fell out of vogue?

I'm not naïve enough to think that requiring kids to keep copybooks will cure all of society's ills. I do believe, however, that for everyone, a return to the truths of the copybooks would go a long way toward fixing things.

Rudyard Kipling wrote about a kind of never-ending warfare between "The Marketplace" and "The Copybook." In a poem titled "The Gods of the Copybook Headings" he argues that people have always been drawn to fads, to pie-in-the-sky philosophies. The human race seems eternally gullible, forever willing to trade hard truth for the quick, easy trend.

Listen to Kipling. He's knows his stuff:

As it will be in the future, it was at the birth of Man,

There are only four things certain since Social Progress began:

That a Dog returns to his Vomit and the Sow returns to her Mire,

And the burnt Fool's bandaged finger goes wobbling back to the Fire:

And that after this is accomplished, and the brave new world begins,

When all men are paid for existing, and no man must pay for his sins,

As surely as Water will wet us, as surely as Fire will burn,

The Gods of the Copybook Headings with terror and slaughter return.

He's saying that, no matter how much "progress" we make, the old truths abide. A dog will return to his vomit. A pig will wallow in the mud. And a fool with burnt fingers will stick them right back into the fire, guaranteed.

Kipling then ends with the best description I've ever read of the modern drift toward moral complacency. We live in a "brave new world," he says, where technology and science have made life so easy that it seems the old rules no longer apply. We live as though we should be "paid for existing," and we act as though "no man must pay for his sins."

But it ain't true, and we're suckers if we think that it is. The Gods of the Copybook Headings persist, whether we recognize them or not. They will be heard from, no matter how deaf we are. Truth is still truth.

Right is still right, and wrong is wrong.

If all of this sounds a little old-fashioned, it is. Who today really talks in terms of "moral precepts"? Certainly not the media; not lawyers or businessmen or doctors. To a large extent (and this is the problem), not even parents or teachers or preachers.

Look, I'm not suggesting that we reject everything new and modern out of hand. Only that we find a little room for ancient wisdom. We'd better, because Rome is burning.

Ash Wednesday

A *middle-aged man knelt at the altar, thinking, remembering, and praying. Of course, he'd knelt there before. Every Sunday for the past year, in fact. But until today he'd never experienced the imposition of ashes. Such seasonal rituals of the church were new to him, their power still fresh, their meaning not yet dulled by years of habit.*

What surprised him most was the grit. He had expected the ashes to be a soft, fine powder, like talc. Instead, for just a moment as the priest marked his forehead, the grit was almost audible: something akin to charcoal on paper or the sound of a finger rubbing against the grain of a five o'clock shadow. He heard and felt it in the bones of his jaw. The priest spoke: "Remember that you are dust, and to dust you shall return."

The sun beat down on the boy's back as he bent over to pull yet another pokeweed. All morning he'd worked, and now the potato patch was littered with the remains of poke, lamb's quarter, thistle and Johnson grass. It didn't take long for the weeds to die, especially if you made the effort to knock the clods of dirt away from the roots. Pokeweed went the quickest. The ones he'd just pulled had already begun to wither in the heat. Tomorrow when he came to the field, the piles he'd left between the rows would have shrunk to dry, gray-green mats.

Just a boy, he had a boy's awareness of time. He thought about the afternoon ahead and counted the remaining rows of potatoes. He thought about the five dollars he'd been promised for doing this job. He thought about what his mother might be fixing for supper. But being a boy, what he didn't think was this: "We fade away suddenly like the grass. In the morning it is green and flourishes; in the evening it is dried up and withered."

The priest passed on to the next supplicant: "Remember that you are dust, and to dust you shall return."

He'd never seen frozen flowers before. Two weeks earlier these arrangements had graced her grave during a funeral conducted in the midst of a massive snowstorm. He'd left the cemetery that day, holding his wife's hand and thinking how beautiful the gladiolus and chrysanthemums had looked against the plump cushion of snow. But now two weeks had passed, and suddenly he remembered that cut flowers couldn't survive the cold. He wondered whether anyone had thought to haul them away. She'd always been one for neatness, and it troubled him to think what two weeks of freezing temperatures might have done to the place.

When he arrived in the old pickup, he winced. Dozens of frozen flower arrangements surrounded the grave. As he began to clear them away, he discovered that the green, water-soaked sponges at the bottom of each basket had frozen into solid blocks of ice. Some weighed as much as ten pounds. One by one, he jerked them from the clumped, red earth and tossed them unceremoniously into the back of the pickup. Ice struck metal with a heavy thud. Tears ran down his cheeks and froze.

The priest passed on: "Remember that you are dust, and to dust you shall return."

He was driving down the road with his two daughters, one seven and one four, when the unanswerable question came. His four-year old, who loved to putter in the flower beds with him, had just asked what it meant to be "buried." What could he say to her that wouldn't frighten? How could he tell her the truth: that when people die, we put them in the ground. Forever. If he told her that, she'd ask if it was dark down there, or if the bugs could get in. There'd be those and a thousand other questions for which he had no suitable answers.

Then, as he struggled for words, came this from his older child: "You know, it's just like planting daffodils. You put them in the ground and they grow." Out of the mouth of babes, true and simple wisdom sufficient for father and daughter alike. He relaxed and breathed again.

The priest moved on, blessing each kneeling petitioner with a cross of ashes on the forehead: "Remember that you are dust, and to dust you shall return."

Lifting his hand, the minister bade them rise. "Go in peace," he commanded. They all stood and left, in peace.